# A CONCISE HISTORY
## OF THE BOOK OF
# COMMON PRAYER

## AN APPRECIATION OF ANGLICANISM

## GARY NICOLOSI

iUniverse®

**A CONCISE HISTORY OF THE BOOK OF COMMON PRAYER**
**AN APPRECIATION OF ANGLICANISM**

*iUniverse books may be ordered through booksellers or by contacting:*

*iUniverse*
*1663 Liberty Drive*
*Bloomington, IN 47403*
*www.iuniverse.com*
*844-349-9409*

*ISBN: 978-1-6632-2509-2 (sc)*
*ISBN: 978-1-6632-2508-5 (e)*

*Library of Congress Control Number: 2021915146*

*Print information available on the last page.*

*iUniverse rev. date: 07/29/2021*

# CONTENTS

# I DEDICATE THIS BOOK

*In Memory of My Parents*
*Joseph and Carol*

*With Continuing Affection for My Wife and Daughter*
*Heather and Allison*

*In Thanksgiving for the People, Parishes and Dioceses*
*I Have Been Blessed to Serve as a Priest*

*And to Greg Thompson, Ken Andrews and Stephen Adams –*
*for Their Support and Encouragement in Writing This Book*
*and Sharing with Me a Love of Our Anglican Heritage*

# PREFACE

I first encountered *The Book of Common Prayer* when I was a twenty-two-year-old graduate student at Georgetown University in Washington, D.C. Back in January 1973, friends invited me to attend Evensong at the Washington National Cathedral. I was reluctant to go. After all, I was raised a Roman Catholic and had never in my life attended any other church. I went out of courtesy, grit my teeth, and kept saying to myself, "It is only one hour and it will be over." Little did I know that I would be awestruck by the worship that Sunday afternoon. I experienced what Rudolf Otto termed, a *"mysterium tremendum."*[1] There, in the Prayer Book service was worship in the beauty of holiness that conveyed to me a deep sense of belonging to the God who is there. I encountered God not from the top of my head but from the depths of my heart. I felt grasped by God, embraced, enraptured and overwhelmed by a personal, powerful presence that claimed me. As the service ended, I knew I was home. That December I was received into the Episcopal Church.

Have you ever had an experience like that, a defining moment that changed your life – a moment when passion welled up deep within you – a moment of fire and cloud when God spoke to you, claimed you, called you – a "shining moment of remembered days" as the poet Gerald Manley Hopkins put it? That was my first encounter with *The Book of Common Prayer*. Since then, I have become an Episcopal priest, served parishes in the United States and Canada, baptized, married and buried countless individuals, presided at Morning and Evening Prayer on Sundays and during the week, celebrated Holy Communion more times than I can count, and ministered to both believers and seekers, drawing them into the presence of God.

*The Book of Common Prayer* is part of the genius of Anglicanism. It makes possible a church not only as a haven for the committed but a shelter for seekers. You can read the words of the Prayer Book and be drawn into an experience of God without any need of certainty or conformity of thought. You can enter into the mystery of God and leave doubtful things doubtful without any requirement that you must believe things in just the right way. I have come to appreciate this readiness to take in all kinds of people as more than merely sensible. It is Christian. The very inclusiveness of the Prayer Book allows room for love to seep through.

*A Concise History of the Book of Common Prayer* originated as a series of lectures I delivered at St. James Westminster Church in London, Ontario in 2012. After I moved to the Phoenix, Arizona region in July 2016, I led a seminar on the history of the Prayer Book at the Church of the Advent in Sun City West, Arizona. That led to being invited to lead a weekend retreat for the St. Timothy's Episcopal Church Men's Group at the San Damiano Retreat Center in Danville, California. Somehow the handouts from that retreat got into the hands of several clergy, and one of them suggested that I write a study manual for use in Episcopal parishes. At first, I wasn't sure if such a book was needed. However, I discovered that while there are books introducing the 1979 *Book of Common Prayer*, there was none on the history and development of the Prayer Book from the sixteenth century to the present time that were suitable for parish study groups. This book is intended to fill the gaps.

The Prayer Book is more than a worship resource, a book of private devotions, or even a Missal. It is a book that shapes the Episcopal way of being Christian, allows a diverse people to worship together, to eat and drink spiritual food at a common table, to hear and reflect on Holy Scripture, and to go out into the world in the power of God's love.

*A Concise History of the Book of Common Prayer* is designed for parish study groups that want to explore Anglican worship, history and theology. However, the book will prove a useful resource for anyone considering becoming a member of a church in the Anglican Communion, particularly in the United States or Canada. It also will be helpful to any Christian or seeker who wants to explore the liturgical richness of the Prayer Book, its prayers, rites and ceremonies, all designed to draw worshipers into an experience of God.

Structurally, *Concise History* is made up of an introduction, ten sessions, final reflections and an appendix. Each session could be discussed a week at a time, or a group could spend two or three weeks on one session. A session could be as brief as forty-five minutes, allowing the class to be offered between Sunday worship services. Or, if conducted weekly, sessions could be offered for an hour or even an hour and a half. Participants should read the material ahead of time and be prepared to discuss it in the group. At each meeting, the facilitator should begin with an overview of the session. Three questions are provided for discussion. These "starter" questions are designed to stimulate conversation. There also are box inserts throughout the book to encourage further discussion.

I have occasionally updated the spelling of the Prayer Books and the writings of the authors cited, but have sought to maintain the language as much as possible, with occasionally updating words or grammar that may not be understood today.

'Church' is capitalized when it refers to a specific institution such as the Church of England or the Roman Catholic Church. When in the lowercase, 'church' refers to the local church, the universal church, or a generic church without specific denominational identity.

The book uses the words 'Anglican' and 'Episcopalian' interchangeably. Most churches of the Anglican Communion identify themselves as Anglican, but some use the word Episcopal. The difference is historical rather than substantive. The word Anglican can be traced back to at least 1246 to refer to the English church – *ecclesia anglicana*. In its original usage, it refers to the Catholic Church in England. At the time of the Reformation, when the Church in England became the Church of England, the word Anglican was not used. The word may have been used as early as 1598, but it was not a common term until the nineteenth century when it began to be used to refer to the Church of England and churches in communion with it. Today these churches are jointly known as the Anglican Communion.

The word 'Protestant' is used to describe the Church of England. I realize that some Anglicans would prefer the term 'reformed Catholic' or even 'Catholic' but I think 'Protestant' is more accurate and in keeping with the self-understanding of the churches of the Anglican Communion until the latter part of the nineteenth century. 'Protestant' was first used by German Lutheran princes and cities in 1530 to defend freedom of conscience against an edict of the Diet of Speyer in 1529 intended to suppress the Lutheran movement. Continental Lutheran and Reformed churches began using the term in the sixteenth century to differentiate their teachings from the Roman Catholic Church.

In 1953, Queen Elizabeth, in her Service for the Coronation, was asked by the Archbishop: "Will you to the utmost of your power maintain in the United Kingdom the Protestant Reformed Religion established by law?" Her answer was, "All this I promise to do."

'Protestant' is often considered a word of protest when it actually affirms Reformation principles of justification by faith alone, the priesthood of all believers, and the primacy of the Bible. Protestant churches also denied the universal authority of the Pope. In this sense, the newly reformed Church of England viewed itself as Protestant. In the late eighteenth century, when the Episcopal Church in the United States was organized, the founders took as the title of their church: the Protestant Episcopal Church in the United States of America – PECUSA. 'Protestant' distinguished the church from Rome while 'Episcopal' signified commitment to the historic episcopate.

'Evangelical' is used extensively in this book, but the word may have negative connotations for some people, especially if associated with right-wing political activism and fundamentalist Christianity. That is not how Anglican evangelicals would understand themselves. Technically the word comes into popular usage with the eighteenth century Great Awakening led by George Whitefield and John Wesley. Towards the end of the eighteenth and first part of the nineteenth centuries, the Cambridge pastor Charles Simeon was an influential leader of evangelical Anglicanism. In the latter part of the nineteenth century, Bishop J.C. Ryle of the Diocese of Liverpool was an articulate apologist for evangelicalism. In the twentieth and twenty-first centuries many prominent priests and bishops of the Church of England would describe themselves as evangelical, including John Stott, Michael Green, and three Archbishops of Canterbury: Donald Coggan, George Carey and Justin Welby.

Most Anglicans in the sixteenth and seventeenth centuries would not have thought of themselves as evangelicals but reformed Christians – part of the great Reformed movement pioneered by Huldrych Zwingli, Heinrich Bullinger, John Calvin and Theodore Beza. Reformed (and Lutheran) Christians affirmed faith alone, grace alone, Christ alone, Scripture alone and glory to God alone. In many ways, these are the five pillars of Protestant theology, and the leaders of the Church of England would affirm all of them.

Evangelicalism, on the other hand, has its roots in eighteenth century revivalism. It is more experiential and conversionist. Anglican theologian J.I. Packer has written that evangelicals stress the supremacy of Scripture, the majesty of Jesus Christ, the lordship of the Holy Spirit, the necessity of conversion (instantaneous or gradual) and new birth, the priority of evangelism, and the importance of fellowship.[2] Other evangelicals would add the substitutionary atonement of Christ.

While there are differences between reformed and evangelical Anglicans – not every reformed Anglican is evangelical nor is every evangelical Anglican reformed – both groups would agree that there is a spiritual but real presence of Christ in the Lord's Supper to every faithful communicant, but no local corporal presence in the bread and wine. Bishop Ryle put it succinctly when he wrote: "But we by the real spiritual presence of Christ do understand Christ to be present, as the Spirit of God is present, in the hearts of the faithful by blessing and grace; and this is all we mean."[3]

Presenting the facts in a coherent and objective narrative is a challenge for any historian. While *The Book of Common Prayer* has been instrumental in my life, and I value the Anglican way of being Christian, my purpose in writing a *Concise History* is not to spin the facts to reach a particular conclusion but to offer an accurate and fair history of the book.

Those who study seriously the history of *The Book of Common Prayer* recognize that it is not really one book but a series of books developed over the centuries, each with its own unique theological emphasis and pattern of worship. In addition, each church of the Anglican Communion has its own Prayer Book. Thus, the Prayer Book is an evolving, living worship book that grows and develops according to context, culture and theology. There is no fixed Prayer Book, only a book for a particular time and people. The Prayer Book is not a Platonic idea come down from the heavens, but the work of men (and today women) who sought to provide a worship book to the church. Although the book may draw us closer to God, it is the work of human beings with all their faults and imperfections as well as their ability to inspire and edify. In many cases, especially in the Episcopal Church, the Prayer Book is the result of a highly political process of discussion, debate and compromise. Charles Mortimer Guilbert, the former custodian of the *American Episcopal Book of Common Prayer,* got it right when he observed that the Prayer Book is whatever General Convention says it is.

Even so, *The Book of Common Prayer* is a gift to the whole church. It is not a book that belongs in a museum but is used in churches today where the Spirit of God inspires and empowers worshippers to love and serve the Lord.

When I was a young priest serving at the Cathedral Church of the Nativity in Bethlehem, Pennsylvania, we had just concluded Choral Morning Prayer. As parishioners were leaving the church, one woman came up to me and said, "Every time I come to church and hear the words of the Prayer Book combined with the singing of the choir, I leave a little stronger, a little more ready to face the world another day, another week."

I like that woman's image of Prayer Book worship as strength to face the world because we have a glimpse of a new world where human beings are reconciled to God and brought into harmony with one another. Through the Prayer Book we experience love, mercy, compassion and the forgiveness of our great God.

*The Book of Common Prayer* will continue to gift the church provided Episcopalians and Anglicans remain faithful stewards in passing it on to future generations. The Prayer Book is a treasure in an earthen vessel, but still a treasure.

# INTRODUCTION

*I BELIEVE there is no LITURGY in the World, either in ancient or modern language, which breathes more of a solid, scriptural, rational Piety, than the COMMON PRAYER of the CHURCH of ENGLAND. And though the main of it was compiled more than two hundred years ago, yet is the language of it, not only pure, but strong and elegant in the highest degree. – John Wesley, Foreword in The Sunday Service of the Methodists in North America (1784)*

*We are not another Church, started up, but the same which before from the Apostles' times held the common and necessary grounds of faith and salvation; which grounds being in latter ages perverted and overturned by Anti-Christianism, have been by valiant champions for the faith of Christ therefrom vindicated, who have only pruned the Lord's vine, and picked out the stones and driven the boats out of his vineyard, but have not made either one or other new. – Bishop Edward Reynolds, An Explication of the Hundred and Tenth Psalm (1632)*

When I was a priest serving a parish in Lancaster, Pennsylvania, a young woman would come to worship with us, always sitting in the last pew. Karen was a seeker with no commitment to any church. However, she was drawn to the Episcopal liturgy and specifically to *The Book of Common Prayer*. One Sunday I spoke to her after the service. "So what brings you to St. Thomas?" I asked her.

"A feeling," she said. "A feeling of being drawn into something, someone, a feeling of which I wasn't really aware until last Sunday."

"Last Sunday?" I asked.

"Last Sunday when everyone was saying the prayer after communion. We were saying those words about being members of the Body of Christ and heirs of God's eternal kingdom. I just got taken up."

"Take up?" I asked.

"Yes. Like taken away. Like I lost consciousness, or maybe gained consciousness. I felt bathed in this warm, wonderful light. As the service ended, I regained my composure and I knew, I really knew, that I believed in Jesus because Jesus believed in me."

Karen's experience is not all that uncommon. *The Book of Common Prayer* has a way of touching the soul like few other books. I have had people who hardly ever attend church come approach me after a marriage service and say, "That service was beautiful. The words really touched me." I have heard the same thing at funerals. One young man said to me, "I haven't been a very faithful Christian but the words of the Prayer Book have challenged me to rethink my faith." I also have had two Presbyterian pastor friends tell me that, outside the Bible, the *Book of Common Prayer* is the greatest treasure in Christendom. And then, there was the business executive who was dying. He lived a life of great success. His home was filled with exquisite furniture, priceless art and an extensive library. However, as he grew weaker and death drew near, there were only two books on his bedside table: his Bible and the Prayer Book.

There is something about *The Book of Common Prayer* that we cannot ignore or dismiss. It is not just a book about God. Rather it is a book which draws us into an encounter with God. We experience the God who is there, the God who in Jesus saves us from our sins, loves us unconditionally, and calls us into his companionship.

The Prayer Book can be tough on us. It calls us to repent of our sins and amend our lives, to confess the wrongful things we have done and left undone. It bids us to take an honest look at ourselves, to acknowledge "our wretchedness" and to admit we are "miserable offenders" but then to go to God asking for forgiveness, knowing that God pardons more than we "desire or deserve." We are justified but sinners, saved but always being saved, by the God who loves us always and forever.

*The Book of Common Prayer*, the works of Shakespeare, the *Authorized* or *King James Version of the Bible*, along with Chaucer's *Canterbury Tales* and the old-English epic *Beowulf* are the most influential works in the English language. Shakespeare is still read today, and his plays continue to be performed in theaters to packed audiences. The *King James Version of the Bible* is still read by some Protestants, and its influence continues in modern translations such as the *Revised Standard Version*, the *New Revised Standard Version*, the *New International Bible* and the *English Standard Version*. *Beowulf* and Chaucer's *Canterbury Tales* continue to be studied in schools and universities to this day.

However, unlike those works, *The Book of Common Prayer* is not a fixed, static book but a living, dynamic worship book that has gone through many revisions around the world. The 1549 Prayer Book was the first, and therefore holds a special place in Anglican history. However, that book was quickly replaced by the 1552 Prayer Book which lasted less than a year before being outlawed by Queen Mary, a devout Roman Catholic. Upon the Queen's death, and with the ascendancy of her half-sister Elizabeth to the throne, the 1559 Prayer Book became the official worship book in the realm. Modified slightly in 1604, the 1559 book became the basis of the 1662 Prayer Book which remains the official worship book of the Church of England, though it is now supplemented by *Common Worship* and other liturgical resources.

After the American Revolution, Episcopalians in the United States compiled their own *Book of Common Prayer*, which was similar but not identical to the English book. One significant difference was that the Eucharistic Prayer was taken from the Episcopal Church of Scotland's 1764 *Book of Common Prayer*. That book used the 1549 Eucharistic Prayer. Canada, on the other hand, in formulating its own Prayer Book in 1893, remained faithful to the rites and ceremonies of the Church of England. However, in its 1962 Prayer Book, the Anglican Church of Canada diverged from the 1662 Prayer Book and developed its own Eucharistic Prayer along the same pattern as The Alternative Order of the Communion in the *1928 Proposed Book of Common Prayer* of the Church of England – a book that was rejected by the British Parliament.

With the advent of liturgical renewal after Vatican II, Anglican churches throughout the world began to develop their own liturgies. Some were conservative revisions of the 1662 Prayer Book, but others, like *A New Zealand Prayer Book* were more radical. Today, Anglican liturgy is quite varied, though there is a common structure in all of them. Still, what makes Anglican liturgy 'Anglican' is a subject of debate. The idea of one Prayer Book for everyone everywhere is no longer practical nor possible. Computers, tablets, the Internet and the digital age have made fixed forms of worship impossible to maintain. We live at a time when priests in the United States and Canada could easily borrow prayers or even full liturgies from Kenya, South Africa, Nigeria, Australia, New Zealand or anywhere else in the world where there is an Anglican presence.

All this begs the question: Is there any such thing as a *Book of Common Prayer*? For now, I want the reader to think through the development of the different Prayer Books from 1549 to the twenty-first century. What you will see is not simply different words, or forms, or structures to the different liturgies, but also different theologies, sometimes slight and unnoticeable, but at other times more pronounced. The history of *The Book of Common Prayer* reflects the different theologies within Anglicanism over the course of centuries.

However, regardless of differing theologies, if you want to know what Anglicans believe, look to the Prayer Book. What Anglicans believed in the sixteenth century is not necessarily what they believe in the twenty-first century. A development of doctrine is apparent in the different books. Sacramental theology today is certainly not identical with that taught by the sixteenth century English reformers, nor is ecclesiology the same since no church in the Anglican Communion except England has the Monarch as the Supreme Governor of the Church. We live in a different world, minister in a different social context, and therefore our theology and worship will be different from that of previous generations. The English reformers understood this need for change, allowed for it, and even expected it. To them, the Reformation was not a 'once for all' event but an ongoing process of church renewal – *ecclesia reformata, semper reformanda* – the church reformed, always reforming.

The idea of liturgical development was anticipated in the Preface to the 1549 *Book of Common Prayer*: "There was never any thing by the wit of man so well devised, or so surely established, which (in continuance of time) hath not been corrupted: as (among other things) it may plainly appear by the common prayers of the Church, commonly called divine service…" The first Prayer Book was an attempt at liturgical renewal: being faithful to the practices of the church in the early centuries of Christian history, taking into account the theological reform on the European continent, and producing understandable and simplified worship services for clergy and laity.

No book written by human beings will ever be timeless, even if its themes are eternal. Language changes, culture changes, the meaning of words change, and what is vernacular in one generation is foreign to another. The Dean of Norwich Cathedral, Humphrey Prideaux, noted in a letter to a friend published in 1690, that with liturgy there was a constant "necessity of correction." Language itself dictated as much. He wrote:

> For nothing of human composure can be such, especially in a thing of this nature, where process of time and alteration of circumstance frequently produce a necessity of correction, as most certainly in our Liturgy they very often do. For the language in which it is written being constantly in flux, as all the living languages are, in every age some words that were in use in the former grow obsolete, and some phrases and expressions formerly in grace and fashion through disuse become uncouth and ridiculous; and always to continue these in our Liturgy without correction would be to bring a disparagement upon the whole and expose to contempt the worship of God among us.

In addition, he noted that human sensibilities also change over time:

> Besides, there are several things which in one age may conduce to devotion which, through variation of times and circumstances, may not be borne in another; several things which may be the proper matter of prayer at one time, which may not be so in another; and all those things call for alterations and amendments whenever they happen.[1]

Dean Prideaux's letter echoed the Preface to the 1662 *Book of Common Prayer* which declared that the "Church, upon just and weighty considerations… hath yield to make such alterations in some particulars, as in their respective times were thought convenient: Yet so as that main Body and Essentials of it… have still continued the same unto this day, and do yet stand firm and unshaken…"

> Changing forms, language, and even rites and ceremonies that no longer speak to the present generation but maintaining the essentials of faith – this has been the challenge of Anglicanism over the centuries.

Liturgical change continues to be deeply relevant to Anglicans today: to have a book that connects to the contemporary culture, but upholds the time-tested truths and heritage of Christian faith. Maintaining this balance is a challenge, to say the least. The church is not a museum that cultivates the old for the sake of reverencing antiquity. It must speak to the world of today in ways that communicate and connect with culture, or its forms of worship risk becoming unintelligible and anachronistic. And yet, it must always proclaim the truth of the Gospel with boldness and conviction.

In delightful language, the Preface to the 1662 Prayer Book recognized this challenge. It begins by saying: "It hath been the wisdom of the Church of England, ever since the first compiling of her Public Liturgy, to keep the mean between two extremes of too much stiffness in refusing, and of too much easiness in admitting, any variation from it." The reason for this balance is to maintain "the peace and unity in the Church."

How peace and unity can be maintained in a world of constantly changing Prayer Books, both official and unofficial, is an issue that Anglicans have yet to resolve. My hope is that as you study the historical development of the Prayer Book, and recognize that there have been many Prayer Books over the centuries reflecting different ways of expressing and affirming faith, you will become more comfortable with diversity in unity and accept that the Prayer Book is not a relic of the past with no relevance to the present, but a living, dynamic worship book that communicates the personal, powerful presence of our great God.

*A Concise History of The Book of Common Prayer* is organized into ten sessions, moving chronologically from pre-Reformation origins to 1662. There are then two sessions on Eucharistic presence and sacrifice – the two central issues that have divided Catholics and Protestants. The book concludes with histories of the American and Canadian Prayer Books, the Oxford Movement and liturgical renewal, the future of a Prayer Book church in our rapidly changing world, followed by final reflections that summarize the course.

***Session 1: Prayer Book Origins*** covers the period prior to 1549, provides the context for the book, and introduces the reader to the key political and religious personalities who shaped the English Reformation. This was a period of enormous intellectual ferment when the monolithic power of the Roman Catholic Church came crashing to the ground. As the American writer Joan Didion put it: "When the ground starts shaking, all bets are off."

***Session 2: The 1549 Book of Common Prayer*** begins with the death of King Henry VIII in 1547 and the ascendancy of the boy-king Edward VI to the throne. Protestants control the government and Archbishop Thomas Cranmer and others initiate church reform. The result is the first *Book of Common Prayer* in 1549 – in many ways more Lutheran than Reformed, but a harbinger of things to come. No one was really happy with the 1549 Prayer Book, and so it was inevitable that the book would be short-lived and another to replace it.

***Session 3: The 1552 Book of Common Prayer*** reflects Cranmer's mature thought as a convinced Zwinglian who rejected the sacrifice of the Mass and the real presence of Christ in the bread and wine of Holy Communion. The evidence is compelling that the 1552 Prayer Book was Reformed theology in liturgical form. And yet, there is an anomaly in the book which is difficult to explain. Despite the Protestant character of the book, the Threefold Order of Ministry is maintained – and even the word 'priest' is used when other words would have sufficed, such as presbyter, pastor or elder. By maintaining bishops, priests and deacons, and by steadfastly continuing the historic episcopate, the Church of England would become a hybrid church with Reformed theology balanced by Catholic order.

***Session 4: The 1559, 1604 and 1637 Prayer Books*** begin with the reign of Queen Elizabeth I and end with the executions of Archbishop William Laud and King Charles I. In some ways, the 1559 Prayer Book, part of what is termed 'the Elizabethan Settlement,' is the most important of the early Prayer Books. Its compilers sought to placate Catholics while maintaining Reformed theology. The Puritans, however, were not satisfied with the book, and many wanted no book at all. The tension in the church would continue and finally explode under Archbishop William Laud and King Charles I. While some commentators claim that Laud and Charles had Catholic sympathies, they, in fact, disliked Roman Catholicism, deemed it 'un-English' and contrary to the emerging European nationalism. And yet, Laud and Charles liked ceremony and ritual done decently and in order, and therefore supported Catholic reverence, form and solemnity while maintaining a Protestant church.

*Session 5: The 1662 Book of Common Prayer* came into existence with the ascendancy of Charles II to throne. This is the book that is still in existence in the Church of England, and more than any other book has shaped the theology and worship of the churches of the Anglican Communion. Its compilers corrected excesses and even errors in previous books, and sought that balance between Reformed theology and Catholic order. The result is a book that is Catholic and Reformed at one and the same time – what some commentators call 'reformed Catholicism.' Others classify it as reflecting a moderate Calvinism. The book represents the best thinking of the Reformation while adhering to the time-tested truths of Catholic faith and order.

*Session 6: What the Reformation Was All About: Eucharistic Presence and Sacrifice* explores the central division between Roman Catholics and Anglicans: the Eucharist. What difference does it make whether the Mass is a sacrifice or a supper? Why does it matter whether the real presence of Christ is spiritual or corporal, a meal of praise and thanksgiving for Christ's 'once for all' sacrifice on the cross, or a renewal of that sacrifice present on the altar through the actions of the priest? Does the priest have the power to remit the sins of the living and the dead by saying Mass? Both Roman Catholics and Anglicans speak for themselves, through the decrees of the Council of Trent, the Articles of Religion, and other sources.

**Session 7: Eucharistic Presence and Sacrifice in Ecumenical Dialogue** deals with attempts since the nineteenth century to bridge the gap between Roman Catholicism and Anglicanism on the Eucharistic doctrines of real presence and sacrifice. The efforts at reconciliation have been, quite frankly, frustrating. Despite significant advances in ecumenical relations, Anglican Orders are still deemed "absolutely null and utterly void" by the Roman Catholic Church. As Bishop Hugh Montefiore put it in the title of his book, Roman Catholics and Anglicans are "so near yet so far." The gap persists, the disagreements have not been resolved, and the controversies of the sixteenth century Reformation continue to cast a shadow over our twenty-first century ecumenical dialogues.

**Session 8: The American and Canadian Books** summarizes the history of the Prayer Books in the United States and Canada. The origin of the American Prayer Book after independence from Britain was the result of intense debate led by two founding members of the Episcopal Church: Samuel Seabury and Willian White. To understand the disagreements between these two men is to begin to grasp the controversies that continue in that church today. The Anglican Church of Canada, on the other hand, has been more intellectually homogenous and, as one would expect from the descendants of the Loyalists, less prone to deviate from the worship and theology of the Church of England. Still, the 1962 *Book of Common Prayer* saw the Anglican Church of Canada come into maturity, with a worship book reflecting a distinct Canadian spirit. Unfortunately, as the book was being praised as a leap forward in Anglican liturgy, Vatican II was just beginning and would initiate a major liturgical renewal that would affect all churches worldwide.

**Session 9: The Oxford Movement and Liturgical Renewal** begins in the early nineteenth century with a movement that would profoundly shape the Anglican Communion. The Oxford Movement originally wanted the Church of England to affirm its Catholic identity in the face of the decision by the British Government to disestablish the Church of Ireland. However, over time the movement began to focus on liturgy, architecture, and ceremony, upholding the church of the Middle Ages as a religious ideal and disparaging the Reformation. 'Catholic, just not Roman Catholic' became a common way for Anglo-Catholics to describe themselves. Although several prominent Anglicans became Roman Catholics, most others remained in the Church of England and sought its reform. Eventually, Holy Communion was celebrated every Sunday in most parish churches in England and around the world. New forms of worship were formulated, and especially after Vatican II there was a proliferation of new Prayer Books in contemporary language and idiom, reflecting the church's effort to connect with an emerging secular culture. And yet, despite the hopefulness of the liturgical renewal movement, churches in North America and the United Kingdom declined dramatically beginning in the mid-1960s, even as the liturgical movement gained momentum and influence.

**Session 10: The Future of Prayer Book Worship** bids us to look at past practices in light of future possibilities. What role does the Prayer Book have in a rapidly changing world where human knowledge doubles every eighteen months and the digital world has replaced print for Millennials and Generation Z? Should our worship be somewhat anachronistic, reflecting time-tested truth and heritage, or should worship be fresh and relevant, connecting with people who increasingly do not know the language or story of Christianity? Increasingly, one hears that the Anglican liturgy is too complex, too formal, and too unintelligible for a growing number of people in Canada and the United States. Young people, in particular, seem to get bored with rote liturgy that is repeated week after week. How do we reach people who grew-up in a digital world and do not think outside the box but beyond the box? Is the Prayer Book part of the answer or is it a hindrance? This session suggests there is a place for the Prayer Book in today's culture so long as church leaders allow for alternative forms of worship to meet people at their own level of need and understanding. In other words, we need to move beyond either/or thinking and be a church grounded in scriptural truth and tradition but soaring freely into a new, emerging world. Faithfulness and flexibility must go together.

**Final Reflections** deals with the heart of the matter about any Prayer Book – the underlying theology that makes Anglican worship Anglican. While Cranmerian language and forms of worship may need to change to meet the challenges of a rapidly changing culture, the church should hold fast to classical Anglican theology. Whether we call that theology reformed Catholicism or moderate Calvinism, it has shaped the church and its identity since the sixteenth century. It is reflected most fully in the 1662 *Book of Common Prayer* which, I submit, should continue to be the standard for all Prayer Books.

*Appendix: An Updated and Condensed Version of the Order of Administration of the Lord's Supper or Holy Communion according to the 1552 Book of Common Prayer* requires an explanation. Why 1552? Why not 1559 which lasted, with some slight modifications, for about one hundred years? Or 1662 which remains the official Prayer Book of the Church of England? These are important books, but there is good reason to give special treatment to the 1552 Communion rite. For one thing, the 1559 and 1662 books are based on the 1552 book. In fact, almost every Prayer Book in Anglicanism is in some way shaped by the 1552 book. Yes, 1552 represents an Anglicanism that is more Zwinglian than moderate

Calvinist, but it reflects the English reformers thinking on the Eucharist. This thinking would carry over to the seventeenth century Anglican divines and is with us still in the reformed and evangelical presence in worldwide Anglicanism. To better appreciate the 1552 Communion rite, I have updated some of the language and condensed parts of the service without, I hope, doing any injustice to the original text. Cranmer was a master of the English language but he could be verbose. Even so, the 1552 book is a shining light of Reformed liturgy. The 'miracle' is not with the transformation of the bread and wine into the Body and Blood of Christ, but with the worthy receivers of the sacrament who become the Body of Christ in the world. The climax of the service is not with the priest pronouncing the words of consecration over the elements, but with Christ present in each individual who receives the elements by faith. At a time when we are far too casual in our reception of communion, the 1552 service bids us to be ready to receive Christ into our hearts by faith – our offering and sacrifice to God.

We are living in a world far different from 1552. It makes no sense to try to repeat the past in present day North America. In any case, Cranmer and the other English reformers would not want us to do that, since they understood that reform, including liturgical reform, is an ongoing process made necessary by a changing cultural and theological context. In a secular age where Christianity is under attack, and the church is in decline in North America and Europe, we need to rethink how we do church, our worship, our ministries, and our mission and outreach. Whether 'worship evangelism' fits into a Prayer Book church is an issue we need to explore. New language, new ways of connecting with a rapidly changing culture need to be balanced by time-tested truth and our Anglican heritage. Can Anglicanism be a relevant, dynamic and vital spiritual movement connecting with new generations that do not know the Gospel adequately or at all, while also proclaiming the faith 'once for all' delivered to the saints? That is the challenge the church faces today.

I continue to believe that the Prayer Book has an important role to play in revitalizing the church and reaching the culture. If we are not too eager to discard what is 'old' but recognize its value for the present, our churches can be bustling centers of faith in a secular culture. Unabashedly preaching the Gospel is part of the answer, but so is being a pastoral church that has a wide embrace for all. Not only can we do both, but Anglicanism is at its best when it reflects both – a solid and substantive faith combined with pastoral sensitivity and openness to all people.

When I was a young priest, my mother went into the hospital for exploratory surgery. The doctor came out of the operating room and told us, "We opened her up; saw all the cancer, then closed her up again. There is nothing we can do." As the news sank into our hearts, we were teary-eyed. My mother knew it was the beginning of the end, and so did I. There were no words adequate to express how we were feeling. I happened to have my Prayer Book and oil with me, and proceeded to anoint her, saying the words that I had said so many times before: "As you are outwardly anointed with this holy oil, so may our heavenly Father grant you the inward anointing of the Holy Spirit." At that moment, both my mother and I felt enormous comfort, because we both knew that whether she lived or died, she would be with the God who loved her.

Three months later, my final act as a priest to my mother was to commend her soul to God. "Into your hands, O merciful Savior, we commend your servant Carol. Acknowledge, we humbly beseech you, a sheep of your own fold, a lamb of your own flock, a sinner of your own redeeming. Receive her into the arms of your mercy, into the blessed rest of everlasting peace, and into the glorious company of the saints in light. Amen."

From ministering to my mother, I have never doubted the power of the Prayer Book to comfort us when we need it most, to express to God words we cannot at the moment express ourselves, to experience the divine assurance that even in the worst of times when we are at our wits' end, God is with us always.

The Prayer Book may not be necessary but it is a highly desirable resource for Christians. With it we are never left to our own strength, our own abilities. Through the words of the Prayer Book, God lifts us up when we cannot lift ourselves. It is miraculous but true. Time and again, people of all backgrounds and conditions have been comforted, strengthened, and inspired by the Prayer Book. Through it they have felt the peace, presence and power of God.

# SESSION 1

## PRAYER BOOK ORIGINS

*I observe that the only way to attain unto the knowledge of the true notion of the Church, is to search into the New Testament, and from the places there which mention it, to conclude what is the nature of it. – Bishop John Pearson, An Exposition of the Creed (1659)*

*For to the Churches of the Roman Communion we can say that ours is reformed; to the Reformed Churches we can say that ours is orderly and decent; for we were freed from the impositions and lasting errors of a tyrannical spirit, and yet from the extravagancies of a popular spirit too. Our Reformation was done without tumult, and yet we saw it as necessary to reform. We were zealous to cast away the old errors, but our zeal was balanced with the consideration and the results of authority... And, indeed, it is no small advantage to our Liturgy that it was the offspring of all that authority, which was to prescribe in matters of religion. – Bishop Jeremy Taylor, An Apology for Authorized and Set Forms of Liturgy (1657 – 1660)*

*The Book of Common Prayer* was a product of its time. It did not just happen. Many different forces in European culture converged for the idea of a common worship book. The Renaissance and Reformation played important roles as did an emerging nationalism in England and a weakened and discredited papacy. A rising merchant and middle class in Europe and a growing individualism led to a desire by some to think and believe freely without restriction or restraint. However, there is one indispensable invention without which *The Book of Common Prayer* would have been impossible – the printing press. It is not unreasonable to claim that the printing press made possible *The Book of Common Prayer.*

The invention of the printing press is credited to Johannes Gutenberg around 1450. It displaced earlier methods of printing and led to the first assembly-line mass production of books. By the end of the fifteenth century, printing presses in operation throughout Western Europe had already produced more than twenty million volumes. In the sixteenth century, with printing presses widespread throughout Europe, their output had increased tenfold to an estimated 150 to 200 million copies. The dissemination of knowledge and new ideas that challenged established authority, had now become possible in ways never before imaginable in the history of civilization.

The printing press revolutionized religion. In fact, it is impossible to conceive of a 'Prayer Book church' or Protestantism whose foundation is the written Word of God in Scripture, without the printing press. In a very real sense, technology made the Reformation and *The Book of Common Prayer* possible. The printing press allowed the widespread dissemination of ideas that otherwise would have been suppressed by the Roman Catholic Church. The same printing press published hundreds of thousands of copies of the Bible and thousands more of *The Book of Common Prayer*.

## I. King Henry VIII

King Henry VIII (1491 – 1547) did not want or lead a reformation of the English church. He was, in fact, a committed Roman Catholic who despised Martin Luther and the continental 'heretics' who were ravishing the church in the early sixteenth century. Henry even wrote a treatise against Martin Luther and the continental Protestants titled *Defense of the Seven Sacraments* for which Pope Leo X (1475 – 1521) declared him "defender of the faith" – a title still used by British monarchs. Although his last wife Catherine Parr (1512 – 1548) was a Protestant, the king's funeral was a Latin Requiem High Mass. So, whether King Henry anticipated a reformation or not, he seemed content to die in the Catholic faith which, for all his faults, he continued to profess.

King Henry was not a Protestant, but he was a committed nationalist intent on maintaining the peace and order of the English nation. When his wife Catherine of Aragon (1485 – 1536) failed to give him a male heir, he feared that England would fall into social and political chaos upon his death. He remembered the destruction that resulted from the War of the Roses at the end of the fifteenth century which brought his father Henry VII to the throne. Henry VIII was determined that another civil war should be avoided at all costs.

Henry's solution was to annul his marriage to Catherine and marry a younger woman who would bear him a male heir. For this, Henry would have to petition the Pope for an annulment. Popes had granted annulments throughout Christian history, and there was an expectation that the present Pope would grant one to Henry.

There was even a biblical basis for the annulment. Henry had married his deceased brother's wife, something forbidden in the Law of Moses: "And if a man shall take his brother's wife, it is an unclean thing: he hath uncovered his brother's nakedness; they shall be childless" (Lev. 20:21, KJV). Henry increasingly came to believe that God had cursed him for marrying Catherine. Although he was not childless – Catherine had given birth to Mary his daughter – he had no son. Thus, he felt cursed.

Henry had his reasons for an annulment, but Catherine was equally adamant in her opposition. She opposed the annulment on the grounds that she and Henry's brother Prince Arthur had never consummated their marriage. The couple was married on November 14, 1501. It was an arranged marriage from the time that Catherine was three years old. At the time of the marriage, Catherine was sixteen and Arthur fifteen. They were married only five months before Arthur died of tuberculosis. Canon and civil law agreed that if a marriage was not consummated, then it is not legally binding. This would have allowed Henry to marry Catherine without any need for a dispensation from the church. It also gave Catherine reason to oppose the annulment.

Cardinal Thomas Wolsey (1473 – 1530), the Chancellor of England, was assigned to obtain the annulment from Rome. However, Pope Clement VII (1478 – 1534) delayed deciding the matter. Rome had been sacked in 1527, and Emperor Charles V (1500 – 1558), the brother of Queen Catherine, threatened to sack Rome again if the Pope issued the annulment. The Pope delayed incessantly until Henry lost all patience. Time was running out; he was getting older; Catherine was beyond childbearing; and the fear of political chaos became more ominous unless there was a male heir to the throne.

Henry had heard of a reticent Cambridge scholar by the name of Thomas Cranmer (1489 – 1556) who had suggested that the King could declare himself the head of the church and break all ties with Rome. Although a good Catholic, Henry was now desperate enough to be open to Cranmer's idea, especially since there seemed little likelihood that the Pope would act on the annulment.

In 1532 Henry appointed Thomas Cranmer as Archbishop of Canterbury, and in 1534, Parliament passed The Act of Supremacy making King Henry VIII "supreme head in earth of the Church of England." The Treason Act made it high treason punishable by death to deny the Royal Supremacy. The Church in England became the Church of England – a national church free of Roman jurisdiction.

Whether Henry knew it or not, Thomas Cranmer was a committed Protestant at the time of his ascendancy to the See of Canterbury. Cranmer annulled the King's marriage to Catherine and presided at his second marriage to Anne Boleyn (1501 – 1536). In 1540 he ordered an English Bible to be placed in every church so that anyone might read it without threat of persecution. This Bible became known as 'The Bishop's Bible' because it was authorized by the bishops of the church with the approval of the King.

Although the English government had severed ties with Rome, suppressed the monasteries and confiscated their wealth, the typical parish church was no different before the schism than after it. The Mass continued to be celebrated in Latin, devotions to the saints continued, the real presence of Christ was adored in the sacrament of the altar, and the seven sacraments continued to be administered as if nothing had changed. Some faithful Catholics such as Sir Thomas More (1478 – 1535) and Bishop John Fischer (1469 – 1535) were executed for their failure to take the oath of allegiance, but most officials, including conservative bishops such as Stephen Gardiner (1483 – 1555), Cuthbert Tunstall (1474 – 1559) and Edmond Bonner (1500 – 1569) accepted the new state of affairs.

Still, even during Henry's reign, there was religious ferment in the kingdom. The Ten Articles of Religion (1536) passed by Convocation with the approval of the King, maintained Catholic orthodoxy on most matters: Baptism imparts remission of sins and regeneration; the Sacrament of Penance is necessary to salvation; the Body and Blood of Christ are really present in the elements of the Eucharist; justification is remission of sin and reconciliation to God by the merits of Christ, but good works are necessary; praying to the saints is permitted; vestments, holy water, candles on Candlemas and ashes on Ash Wednesday are good and laudable; and it is good and charitable to pray for the dead. The Articles rejected images as objects of worship and the efficacy of papal pardons and of soul-masses to remit the sins of the dead. Moreover, only three of the seven sacraments were mentioned in the Articles, which left four uncertain as to their status.

The Ten Articles failed to settle the doctrinal controversies sweeping the land, and so in 1537, the Bishop's Book was issued. The four missing sacraments in The Ten Articles were restored, though placed in a separate section, but justification by faith and the uncertainty of purgatory were maintained. The King was not entirely satisfied with the statement on justification by faith, and as a result, the Bishop's Book was never authorized by the Crown or Convocation.

Continental Lutheran theologians continued to press the Church of England for a clearer statement of Protestant faith. The result was the issuance of The Six Articles in 1539. However, rather than affirm Lutheran theology, The Six Articles affirmed the real presence of Christ in the bread and wine of Holy Communion, rejected communion in both kinds, mandated clerical celibacy and upheld private votive Masses for the dead. Protestants won a small victory in that auricular confession was deemed not mandated by divine law. On the whole, in the face of intense Protestant pressure, England maintained Catholic doctrine. Harsh penalties were attached to violations of the Articles. Denial of transubstantiation was punished by burning without opportunity to recant. Denial of any other articles was punished by hanging or life imprisonment. Married priests were given a brief time to put away their wives before being subject to punishment. The Six Articles would shape Henry's tenure as King until his death. They were finally repealed in 1547 under Edward VI.

> King Henry VIII was a committed Catholic and a nationalist. Although he severed ties with Rome, he never embraced the doctrines of the Protestant Reformation. From a Roman Catholic perspective, Henry may have led the English Church into schism, but he was never a heretic. Throughout his reign, he maintained Catholic faith and order without the Pope.

King Henry VIII would be appalled to think of the Church of England as a "new" church or a church aligned with the continental Protestant churches. Even after he had broken with Rome, he had ordered heretics to be burned at the stake for denying transubstantiation. To him, 'the miracle of the Mass' in which bread and wine were transubstantiated into Christ's Body and Blood was at the heart of the Christian faith. This is why Henry had many loyal conservative supporters among the bishops who expected the Church of England to be a Catholic Church without the Pope. However, as these bishops would soon realize after Henry's death, this would prove untenable given the forces for reform in the kingdom.

## II. King Edward VI

Upon Henry VIII's death, his son Edward VI (1537 – 1553) ascended the throne. However, because Edward was still a young boy, his uncle Edward Seymour became Protectorate, and later John Dudley. With both Seymour and Dudley, the church moved in a decidedly reformed direction.

Archbishop Thomas Cranmer was now able to reform the church in a way not possible under King Henry VIII. Cranmer was influenced and advised by several prominent continental Protestant theologians who came to England to assist in the establishment of a reformed church.

Martin Bucer (1491 – 1551) was perhaps the most influential continental theologian in England, a dear friend of Cranmer and the person who most influenced the 1552 *Book of Common Prayer*. Bucer strongly objected to the idea of the Mass as a sacrifice, rejected liturgical garments, the altar and many Catholic rites and ceremonies. On the real presence of Christ in the Eucharist, Bucer abandoned any idea of a corporal real presence in the bread and wine, and accepted Huldrych Zwingli's interpretation of a spiritual presence only.

A person much different from Martin Bucer was Peter Martyr Vermigli (1499 – 1562). He was an Italian theologian who assumed the position of Regius Professor of Divinity at Oxford. He too influenced the 1552 Prayer Book and rejected both the sacrifice of the Mass and the real presence of Christ in the bread and wine of Holy Communion. Peter Martyr was as much opposed to the Lutheran understanding of sacramental presence as he was to the Roman Catholic doctrine of transubstantiation. He believed, like Zwingli, that Christ's body remains in heaven, even though he is offered spiritually to those who partake of the Eucharist by faith.

Jan Laski (1499 – 1560) was a Polish reformer who went to England and became superintendent of the Strangers' Church in London. Laski had some influence on ecclesiastical affairs during the reign of Edward VI. He argued unsuccessfully for a Reformed model of church government without bishops. He also believed there was no difference between ordained ministers and laity except in terms of who could teach and administer the sacraments.

What Martin Bucer, Peter Martyr Vermigli and Jan Laski had in common was a reliance on the great continental theologians of the Reformation: Martin Luther, Ulrich Zwingli, Heinrich Bullinger and John Calvin.

Martin Luther (1483 – 1546) was the most conservative of the four, especially in his view of the real presence of Christ in the Eucharist. Although there is some question on whether Luther himself taught the doctrine of consubstantiation, he did believe in sacramental union in which Christ was present "in, with and under" the elements of bread and wine. Just as Christ was both God and human, so the sacrament was bread and wine but also Christ's Body and Blood. Luther rejected scholasticism and with it the distinction between substance and accident, but he also believed that when Christ said, "This is my Body," he meant it literally. The bread, though remaining bread, is the Body of Christ. The wine, though remaining wine, is the Blood of Christ. The connection between the bread and wine and the Body and Blood of Christ is mingled together in such a way that they constitute one and the same thing. In this way, Luther rejected scholasticism while maintaining a belief in the real presence of Christ in the elements.

> Scholasticism had its origins in the early twelfth century as a system of philosophy and theology that relied heavily on the classical philosophies of Aristotle and Plato, combined with a strong emphasis on tradition and dogma. The scholastic method employed dialectical and syllogistic reasoning, Aristotelian logic, and knowledge by inference to resolve contradictions. Scholasticism relied on Aristotle's distinction between substance (the thing in itself) and accidents (outward appearance) to explain how bread and wine become the Body and Blood of Christ.

Ulrich Zwingli (1484 – 1531) was a contemporary of Martin Luther but would eventually become his rival, especially on the doctrine of the Eucharist. Zwingli rejected the belief that when Christ said, "This is my Body," he meant it literally. For Zwingli, the bread and wine symbolize but are not really Christ's Body and Blood. At the Lord's Supper, the bread remains bread; the wine remains wine. It is by faith only that we receive Christ spiritually but not corporally. Zwingli's Catholic critics accused him of promoting a theology of 'the real absence,' but his supporters preferred the term 'mystical real presence' – a communion with God and fellow worshippers that transcends physical limitations. Zwingli himself insisted that at the Lord's Supper, the Body of Christ is eaten in a sacramental and spiritual manner by faith. Reception is spiritual not physical, with Christ received in the heart and not in the mouth.

Heinrich Bullinger (1504 – 1575) followed Ulrich Zwingli as head of the Zurich church after Zwingli's untimely death in battle. Although a disciple of Zwingli, in many ways he is far more important because of his extensive writings and nuanced teachings on Reformed doctrine. Bullinger and John Calvin together wrote a response to the Roman Catholic Council of Trent and then a treatise on the Lord's Supper which they hoped would unite Protestants of all persuasions. Although he never visited England, Bullinger had a profound influence on Protestant fugitives fleeing religious persecution during the reigns of Henry VIII and Mary I. His writings found broad distribution in England and continued to be influential long after his death. In 1586, for example, Archbishop John Whitgift (1530 – 1604) ordered all non-graduate ordinands to buy and read Bullinger's *Decades*, a treatise on pastoral theology. Along with Martin Bucer and

John Calvin, Bullinger is perhaps the most influential theologian of the English Reformation.

John Calvin (1509 – 1564) taught a similar doctrine as Zwingli regarding the Eucharist, though he tried to find common ground between the views of Luther and Zwingli through reliance on the Holy Spirit. His doctrine can be summarized by saying that Christ's Body and Blood are received through the Spirit, even though physically or corporally the elements remain bread and wine. Calvin's doctrine is known as the real spiritual presence or pneumatic presence of Christ in the Lord's Supper. Through the Holy Spirit we receive the Body and Blood of Christ by means of bread and wine. Calvin deemed this a miracle beyond rational explanation, a mystery to be believed rather than to be fully understood. What makes Calvin important is his *Institutes of the Christian Religion*. It is the most influential work of the Reformation, laying out systematically reformed Christian teaching in a way that neither Luther nor Zwingli had ever accomplished. Here was the theological justification for the ecclesiastical, liturgical, dogmatic and moral reform of the church – all in one book.

All the reformers claimed the support of the Church Fathers for their teachings. Calvin was convinced Augustine was on his side. Thomas Cranmer, in his treatise on the Lord's Supper, quoted the Church Fathers extensively to support his views. However, Roman Catholics equally claimed the Church Fathers as their own. One of their most brilliant scholars was Cardinal Robert Bellarmine, a Jesuit and adviser to Popes. In one of his homilies, Bellarmine preached: "Let us consider those most burning lights which God hath willed to shine in the firmament of the Church, that all the darkness of heresy might be dispersed, such as Irenaeus, Cyprian, Hilary, Athanasius, Basil, the two Gregories, Ambrose, Jerome, Augustine, Chrysostom, and Cyril. Do not their lives and conduct shine forth in the records which they have left us, as in a special kind of mirror? For out of the fullness of the heart, the mouth speaketh."[1] Clearly, Catholics were not about to allow Protestants to usurp the Church Fathers for their own purposes.

> The irony of the Reformation is that both sides claimed the same sources to support their views. The Church Fathers had such sufficiently diverse writings that Protestants and Catholics could pick and choose the passages that supported their doctrinal positions. St. Augustine, for example, the greatest theologian of the Christian Church, has been called 'the father of all heresies' because his writings can be interpreted to support almost every contentious doctrinal position.

There were other reformers who had an influence on the Prayer Book, including two Roman Catholics. Cardinal Quignon of Spain developed a reformed breviary that was published in Rome in 1535 and included the continuous reading of Scripture and a Confession and Absolution before Matins and Vespers. Archbishop Hermann von Wied of Cologne, who had Lutheran sympathies, published a *Consultation* that included a Litany, Communion and Baptismal Offices, and a Confirmation service, all of which Cranmer used in formulating the first Prayer Book. In addition, the "Comfortable Words" in the Communion Service also is from Archbishop Hermann's *Consultation*. Finally, Valerandus Pollanus, a Calvinist refugee from Strasburg, may have been influential in placing the Ten Commandments into the Communion Service along with the last phrase of the Kyrie, "write all these Thy laws in our hearts." Bishop T.W. Drury suggested that this "is one of the earliest instances of the use of the Decalogue in public worship, and its fitness as a means of coming to the Lord's Table needs no proof."[2]

## III.  A Reformed English Church

After the death of Henry VIII, the Church of England moved steadily into the Protestant camp, at first slowly and incrementally with the 1549 Prayer Book but then decisively with the 1552 book. The worship and faith of the church was rooted in the Bible and the early church, and medieval accretions, superstitions, and devotions to the saints were eliminated. All the English reformers believed that Christ and Christ only is Lord and

Savior, Mediator and Redeemer, whose perfect sacrifice on the cross saves us from the sin from which we cannot save ourselves. We are justified by faith apart from works. Salvation is from first to last by grace, and we are saved by God's initiative and not our merits or deserving. Since this is so, God and God only is worthy of praise, glory and adoration, and it is God who calls us into eternal life with him.

As Archbishop Cranmer pondered how to transfer Reformation doctrine into liturgical form, five principles governed the formation of the first Prayer Book.

First, there was a preference for **simplicity**. Most worship books were incredibly complicated and elaborate. Cranmer wanted a book that both clergy and laity could follow without any difficulty.

Second, there was a desire to **return to the sources** (*ad Fontes*). This was a Renaissance idea to rely on original sources rather than secondary materials, commentaries and interpretations. For Cranmer, this meant a renewed attention to the Bible and the Church Fathers as primary sources of Christian faith. Cranmer, like all scholars of the Renaissance, was convinced that sound knowledge depends on the earliest and most fundamental sources, such as the practices of the early church as opposed to medieval accretions.

Third, Cranmer was resolved to be **faithful to the early church** of the first five centuries. In his book *A Defence of the True and Catholick Doctrine of the Sacrament*, Cranmer is constantly quoting the Church Fathers to support his view of the Eucharist. His intent was never to start a new church, only to reform an existing one. While not rejecting all medieval worship, he eliminated prayers, rituals and ceremonies he believed inconsistent or even a corruption of Scripture and the early church.

Fourth, there was a desire for **uniform worship** in the church. The Roman Catholic Church had many different worship books, and no one book was all-encompassing. These books consisted of the Missal for the Order of Holy Communion; the Manual which contained occasional, pastoral services; the Breviary for the canonical hours read by clergy; the Processional which was a collection of processional services; the Pontifical which were services conducted by a bishop; and the Pie, a rulebook on how to put the various services together. Roman liturgy prior to the Reformation was extremely complex. In addition, England had many different liturgical practices. Religious orders (Benedictine, Cistercian, Carthusian, Franciscan) and different cathedrals (York, Exeter, Hereford, Lincoln, Wells, London and Salisbury) all developed distinctive liturgical traditions, which in turn influenced parishes. The end result was a lack of uniformity in English worship. Cranmer wanted one book of worship for the entire realm.

Fifth, Cranmer introduced the use of the **vernacular** (rather than Latin) in worship. There was a desire by the English reformers that the liturgy should be in the language of the people. They wanted the liturgy to be intelligible to all worshippers, whatever their station in life. The idea of a priest mumbling Latin that could hardly be heard by any worshipper was priestcraft to the reformers. Instead they wanted priest and people to share together in all aspects of worship. Homily 21 of the *Book of Homilies* on the use of the vernacular in common prayer made the case that the early church prayed in their own languages: "Thus are we taught, both by the Scriptures and the ancient doctors, that in the administration of common prayer and sacraments, no tongue unknown to the hearers ought to be used."[3]

Although Cranmer had to implement his reforms very cautiously under Henry VIII, he did order in 1543 that a chapter of the English Bible be read at Matins and Vespers. After the king's death in 1547, he ordered that the epistle and Gospel be read in English, even though the Mass was still in Latin. In 1544, he even issued a Litany for processions which eliminated most of the petitions to the saints, and in 1549, mention of saints was eliminated completely. Liturgical processions were completely ended in 1547.

All these minor reforms were a prelude to a new worship book. In developing the first Prayer Book of 1549, Archbishop Cranmer took the lead, consulting with Bishops representing both sides of the Reformation debate: the reformers, who wanted significant change in the worship of the church, and the traditionalists, who wanted few changes and favored Latin. From all parts of the church, Cranmer combined and blended various features with magnificent prayers that he himself wrote or translated from Latin to English. He used the Bible as the basis for his prayers. Finally, in 1549, the first *Book of Common Prayer* appeared in print.

# Questions

1. If the printing press was indispensable to the Protestant Reformation and *The Book of Common Prayer*, what are the implications for the church today as we deal with a new technological revolution with print becoming digitalized and images supplementing words?
2. We think of the catholic church as universal or global, but it also is local. How does your parish act as both global and local in its ministries?
3. What do you think of Cranmer's five principles for the formation of a Prayer Book? In light of present-day liturgies, how would those principles apply today?

# SESSION 2

# THE 1549 BOOK OF COMMON PRAYER

*Let us therefore so travail to understand the Lord's supper, that we be no cause of the decay of God's worship, of no idolatry, of no dumb massing, of no hate and malice; so may we the boldlier have access thither to our comfort. – An Homily of the worthy receiving and reverent esteeming of the Sacrament of the Body and Blood of Christ, Second Book of Homilies (1563)*

*Therefore, forsaking the corrupt judgment of fleshly men which care not but for their carcass, let us reverently hear and read Holy Scriptures, which is the food of the soul. Let us diligently search for the well of life in the books of the New and Old Testament and not run to the stinking puddles of men's traditions, devised by men's imagination, for our justification and salvation. – Homily on a Fruitful Exhortation to the Reading and Knowledge of Holy Scripture, First Book of Homilies (1547)*

King Henry VIII died in 1547. Throughout his reign, he was a loyal Roman Catholic for the first part of his life and a resolute Catholic for the remainder of his life. Although the Bishop of Rome, the Pope, had no jurisdiction in the English nation, Catholicism continued to flourish in the parishes, with few of the faithful aware of any significant changes. The Mass was in Latin, priests were forbidden to marry, and those convicted of heresy, whether Lutheran, Reformed or Anabaptist, either recanted, fled into exile, or were executed. When King Henry died, the Church of England was Catholic without the Pope.

> A Catholic Church without the Pope is not unique to Anglicanism. The Orthodox Churches of the East have maintained this position since the schism with Rome in 1054 A.D.

It would be inaccurate to say that King Henry VIII had any desire for a religious reformation in England. He severed ties with Rome only so he could annul his marriage to Queen Catherine and marry Anne Boleyn. Through the influence of Thomas Cromwell (1485 – 1540), the King's Viceregent in Spirituals, Henry abolished the monasteries and convents to get their lands and money, but not for religious reasons. Henry was at heart a conservative, both politically and theologically, and he detested the continental Reformation. Although he vacillated between favoring his Catholic and Protestant subjects at Court, throughout Henry's reign, and with some slight changes, the Church of England in most instances remained wedded to similar doctrines and forms of worship as the Church of Rome.

However, when Henry died, he was succeeded by his nine-year-old son Edward VI, son of Jane Seymour (1508 – 1537), Henry's third wife. A committee was immediately formed under Archbishop Cranmer's leadership to produce an entire service book in English. In December 1548, the book was submitted to Parliament for approval; and three months later, in the spring of 1549, printed copies went on sale. While the main text was printed in black, the instructions were in red, and hence became known as "rubrics." The first service of Holy Communion according to the new Prayer Book was celebrated on Pentecost Sunday 1549, at St. Paul's Cathedral.

## I. The Idea of a Book of Common Prayer

The title of the book summarizes its contents: "*The Book of Common Prayer and Administration of the Sacraments and other rites and ceremonies of the Church after the use of the Church of England.*" This book would be like no other worship book in the history of Christianity.

It would be a book of common prayer designed for public use in all churches. It would maintain the word "sacrament" as a continuation of the historic church's use of the word to describe Baptism and the Eucharist (in contrast to Anabaptists who preferred the word "ordinance"). It would include the rites and ceremonies of the church, including the Daily Office of Matins and Evensong. It would ensure that public worship was decent and in order with prescribed requirements for the manner of ritual and ceremonies.

The rationale for the book was laid out in the Preface which began: "There was never any thing by the wit of man so well devised, or so surely established, which (in continuance of time) hath not been corrupted…" In other words, the passage of time makes necessary liturgical reform because rites and ceremonies become corrupted, lose their original meaning, and no longer edify the church.

Moreover, the Preface states the "ancient fathers" are a guide for right worship, intending that the whole Bible (or the greatest part thereof) should be read over once in the year. This was in sharp contrast to the medieval breviaries and office books which read very short portions of the Bible with the exception of reading all 150 psalms every week. Archbishop Cranmer wanted the Old Testament to be read once and the New Testament three times every year.

Since Latin was no longer the common language of the people, the Prayer Book would be in English. The vernacular replaced Latin as the language of worship, though Latin could be used where the congregation understood it. In colleges and universities, for example, where both faculty and students knew Latin, there were occasions when the Latin Prayer Book was used in worship.

There was a great desire that every Christian in England know the Bible, either being read at church or reading it privately at home. Thus, the Preface declared that in public worship that which is to be read is "the very pure word of God, the holy scriptures, or that which is evidently grounded upon the same, and that in such a language and order as is most easy and plain for the understanding, both of the readers and hearers." The intent here is to move away from reading the lives of the saints, tales of miracles and apparitions, or anything else non-biblical. The Bible, the Word of God alone, was to be read in churches, and sermons were expected to be on texts of scripture and not on pious devotions, fables, stories or any other non-biblical source. Of course, preaching effective biblical sermons required a well-trained clergy, and in the transition period of forming such clergy, a *Book of Homilies* was published to assist clergy in their preaching.

Australian Anglican theologian Tim Patrick points out that one major characteristic of *The Book of Common Prayer* "is the heavy use of Scripture throughout. There are many direct quotations of the Bible both brief and extensive, as well as many allusions to Scripture woven throughout the prose."[1] The Prayer Book is saturated in Scripture with an emphasis on the Reformation doctrines of human sinfulness, Christ's once-for-all sacrifice, repentance and forgiveness – all designed to form Christians in the way of the Gospel.

Moreover, *The Book of Common Prayer* was designed as one book for one nation – a way of ensuring that the whole realm shall have "one use" of service. Where there was any question about the use of a service, the Preface ends by saying that such questions shall be brought to the attention of the "Bishop of the Diocese" who shall resolve the matter.

As the Preface made clear, the 1549 Prayer Book was designed to advance reform in a conservative way, emphasizing scripture, simplifying the liturgy and making it intelligible to the common man or woman, reforming but not abolishing the rites and ceremonies of the church, getting rid of medieval accretions while maintaining what is essential to authentic Catholic worship. The book is both Catholic and Protestant. However, it also adheres to the Renaissance maxim *"ad Fontes"* – back to the sources – insisting on scriptural worship that is in accord with the most ancient practices of the church.

> **The English Reformation began as a conservative reform, not a revolution. The goal was to renew the church, not start a new one. Old and new, heritage and learning, time-tested truth and an openness to the Holy Spirit – this is the spirit underlying the 1549 Prayer Book.**

At the heart of the Prayer Book is balance – not clinging to tradition for tradition's sake or discarding everything that is post-New Testament. Past practices would be preserved, if possible; the new learning would be embrace, if desirable. The opening section on Ceremonies, Why Some Be Abolished and Some Reformed gives a sane, balanced rationale for liturgical change which avoids extremes and walks a middle way: "Whereas in this our time the minds of men are so diverse, that some think it a great matter of conscience to depart from a piece of the least of their ceremonies (they be so addicted to their old customs); and again on the other side, some be so new-fangled that they would innovate all things, and so despise the old, that nothing can please them but what is new: it was thought expedient not so much to have respect how to please and satisfy either of these parties, as how to please God and profit them both."

> Cranmer relied significantly on existing church liturgy in writing *The Book of Common Prayer.* He was not intent on overthrowing the liturgical heritage of the church but in reforming it. He also wanted to prevent any unnecessary discomfort or disruption in the parishes. Many of the collects and prayers used on Sundays and in the daily offices, for example, are translations from the Latin. While the services would be in English, continuity with the past was maintained.

## II. The Daily Office

The Daily Office of the 1549 Prayer Book arrived as a work in progress. It was by no means complete. The structure that Anglicans now take for granted was not yet finalized. Glancing at the Offices one might think they are almost an after-thought and of not great importance. The Offices would need more work, but that effort would result in the much-improved 1552 Daily Office. Therefore, it is best to take both the 1549 and 1552 books together when dealing with the Daily Office.

The 1549 *Book of Common Prayer* replaced the seven daily offices of monasticism with two offices – Morning and Evening Prayer. At the heart of the Daily Office was a four-fold structure: 1) Psalms, 2) Lessons, 3) Canticles, and 4) Prayers.

Archbishop Cranmer took the monastic offices of Matins and Lauds and combined them into one service of Morning Prayer. While Matins had two and sometimes three or four readings, both scriptural and non-scriptural, Cranmer replaced them with two biblical readings, one from the Old Testament or Apocrypha and one from the New Testament.

The monastic office of Vespers was replaced by Evening Prayer. While Vespers would have a very short biblical reading of one or two verses, Cranmer instead had two biblical readings, one from the Old Testament or Apocrypha and one from the New Testament. The Old Testament was appointed to be read once through the year and the New Testament three times. While the monastic offices required that all 150 psalms be sung or read each week, Cranmer had all 150 psalms read each month, dividing the Psalter into sixty sections. On those months when there were thirty-one days, the psalms of Day Thirty would be repeated.

The Daily Office of Morning and Evening Prayer reflects the reformed emphasis on a Bible-reading church. Roman Catholics have criticized the Anglican Daily Offices as being too cerebral, too focused on Bible reading and not focused enough on prayer, meditation and contemplation. There may be some truth to this criticism. There is a different feel to the Anglican Daily Office in contrast to the monastic offices. The Anglican Daily Office was designed not just for clergy but for all members of the church. It was an office that could be used by working people with families and not just by monks in a monastery. And yes, it was designed to build up Christians in their knowledge of the Bible, because to the reformers, Scripture was foundational to the church.

## III. Other Prayers, Rites and Ceremonies

In addition to the Daily Office of Morning and Evening Prayer, the 1549 Prayer Book included both old and new prayers, rites and ceremonies revised and shaped with a more reformed theological orientation, but still maintaining enough of the old religion in an attempt to placate traditionalists who were wary of any reforms.

1. **The Great Litany** was designed to supplant a host of medieval church litanies to the Blessed Virgin Mary and the saints. The litany was structured according to prayers of mercy, deliverance and petition, along with a series of collects and suffrages. There were prayers for the king, the bishops, the nobility, and the people of England. There were prayers for the sick, for safe travel, for orphans and widows, for the fruits of the earth, and even "to beat

down Satan from under our feet." But perhaps the most notable petition was one directed against the Pope, who even in 1549 was now considered an enemy of England: "From all sedition and privy conspiracy, from the tyranny of the bishop of Rome and all his detestable enormities, from all false doctrine and heresy, from hardness of heart, and contempt of thy word and commandment: *Good lord, deliver us.*"

2.  The rite of **Baptism** was the most medieval of the services in the 1549 Prayer Book. The rite included an exorcism, the putting on of a white vesture, and an anointing with oil called a chrismation.

    *   **Exorcism:** *Then the minister, looking upon the person to be baptized shall say:* "I command thee, unclean spirit, in the name of the Father, of the Son, and of the Holy Ghost, that thou come out and depart from the person... Therefore, thou cursed spirit, remember thy sentence, remember thy judgement, remember the day is at hand, wherein thou shalt burn in fire everlasting, prepared for thee and thy angels."
    *   **White *Vesture*:** *Then the minister shall put upon the person baptized a white vesture, and say:* "Take this white vesture for a token of the innocence, which by God's grace in this holy sacrament of baptism, given unto thee; and for a sign whereby thou art admonished...to give thyself to innocence of living..."
    *   **Anointing *with Oil*:** *Then the minister shall anoint the person baptized on the head, saying:* "Almighty God, the Father of our Lord Jesus Christ, who hath regenerated thee by water and the Holy Ghost, and hath given unto thee remission of all thy sins: he vouchsafe to anoint thee with the unction of his Holy Spirit, and bring thee to the inheritance of everlasting life."

3.  **Confirmation** was deemed a rite in which adults, young adults or even children had the opportunity to profess Christian faith for themselves that was professed for them by their parents and godparents at their baptism. Although never theologically defined

by a church council, baptism was viewed as incomplete until the candidate professed the Christian faith. The "I believe" said on behalf of the candidate by parents and godparents was now to be professed publicly by the candidate.

The English reformers accepted this medieval understanding of Confirmation but gave it an even more intellectual character, mandating that *"A Catechism, that is to say, an instruction to be learned of every child, before he be brought to be confirmed of the Bishop."* The candidate was expected to rehearse the articles of Christian belief, specifically the Apostles' Creed, the Ten Commandments and the Lord's Prayer. Then the candidate was expected to explain each of them to the bishop in question-and-answer form. The underlying assumption was that to recite the answers in the Catechism indicated that a person had the knowledge to be a Christian, and thus could be confirmed by the bishop – Confirmation being a confirming of the faith of the individual to be a communicant of the church.

Confirmation was more than a rite of passage into adulthood. It was a rite of passage into full communion in the church. To be confirmed meant that one could now receive Holy Communion as the rubric made plain: *"And there shall be none be admitted to the holy communion until such time as he be confirmed."* In this understanding of the sacrament, it was Confirmation and not Baptism that made one a full member of the church, thus able to receive Holy Communion as a communicant in good standing.

4.  **The Form of Solemnization of Matrimony** was a relatively long, wordy service that maintained several medieval practices but also took great care to explain the meaning of matrimony from both the Old and New Testaments. Matrimony was not attached to Holy Communion, so there was no explicit provision for a Nuptial Mass. However, at the end of the rite, there is this rubric: *"The newly married persons (the same day of their marriage) must receive the holy communion."* Whether this meant attendance at Mass or receiving the Reserved Sacrament is left unclear.

5. **Visitation of the Sick** maintained the practices of private confession to a priest and the reservation of the sacrament of Holy Communion with these rubrics:

   • **Private Confession:** *Here shall the sick person make a special confession, if he/she feels his/her conscience troubled with any weighty matter. After which confession, the priest shall absolve him/her after this form; and the same form of absolution shall be used in all private confessions. If there be no priest present, the absolution shall not be said.*

   • **The Reserved Sacrament:** *At the previous celebration of the Holy Communion in the church, the priest shall reserve so much of the sacrament of the body and blood as shall serve sick persons.*

6. **Burial of the Dead** contained a provision for the celebration of Holy Communion. While the rite makes no mention of Purgatory, there are prayers for the dead, including a general commendation to God for the departed and a belief in the resurrection of the dead.

7. **The Order for the Purification of Women** is a service to give thanks for a safe childbirth. At a time when many women died in childbirth, or their infants did not survive, this rite was a way for women to give thanks for their own lives and the lives of their newborns. Despite the title of the rite, "the Purification of Women," the rite had nothing to do with purification but deliverance from the dangers of giving birth.

8. **An Ash Wednesday Commination** was a service without ashes. There were prayers of penitence, a call for self-examination, a long exhortation on the importance of contrition and amendment of life, and prayers that God would have mercy on our sinful selves – but no imposition of ashes. In many ways, the Ash Wednesday service is the most thoroughly reformed of any of the services in the 1549 Prayer Book.

## IV.  The Supper of the Lord, and Holy Communion, commonly called the Mass

I have saved the rite of the Holy Eucharist for last, because it is by far the most controversial part of the 1549 Prayer Book. It was so controversial when introduced into the parishes that it caused a rebellion in Devonshire and Cornwall. It is not an exaggeration to say that the majority of the English people deeply disliked the first Prayer Book. Their Catholic faith and heritage was at stake, and they resented being told they had to worship in a way that they perceived as foreign to their religious sensibilities and even heretical.

There is a great deal of debate on whether the 1549 Eucharist was ever intended to be permanent, or only a first phase towards a more reformed liturgy. In other words, how much weight are we to give to the 1549 Eucharist?

On the face of it, the liturgy appears to be Lutheran with just enough Catholic elements to satisfy the theological conservatives. In many areas, especially in the Eucharistic Prayer, there is sufficient ambiguity to allow for diverse interpretation. Is there still a 'sacrifice of the Mass' or a 'real presence' of Christ's Body and Blood in the consecrated bread and wine? Diehard reformers were not satisfied with the rite, while some traditionalists managed to interpret it in a sufficiently Catholic sense. Church historian and theologian Nigel Scotland has maintained that the 1549 Communion liturgy was "largely based on the Sarum Mass... The most obvious of these was the consecration prayer that still required the priest to place his hands over the bread and over the wine and invoke the Holy Spirit's presence on them... This suggested that it was at that moment of the Spirit's coming upon the elements that they changed in substance."[2] No wonder traditionalists were, grudgingly, prepared to accept the new book.

The 1549 rite allowed for more ceremony than any other Prayer Book until the twentieth century. The rubrics declared that the celebrating priest shall wear *"a white Alb plain, with a vestment or cope."* There is no mention of a stole or chasuble, although some scholars believe that "vestment" may include both. The medieval church viewed the stole and chasuble as symbols of the priesthood but not the alb or cope.

The Order of Communion is, in many ways, more Lutheran than Reformed.

- Collect for Purity
- Lord, have mercy
- Glory be to God on high
- Collects
- Epistle
- Gospel
- Creed
- Sermon
- Offertory
- Preface
- The Prayer and Consecration
- The Lord's Prayer
- The Breaking of Bread
- Confession and Absolution
- Comfortable Words
- Prayer of Humble Access
- Reception of Communion
- Post Communion Prayer
- Blessing

The words of administration reflect a Catholic sense of the real presence of Christ in the Eucharistic elements: "The body of our Lord Jesus Christ which was given for thee, preserve thy body and soul unto everlasting life." "The blood of our Lord Jesus Christ which was shed for thee, preserve thy body and soul unto everlasting life." The service also provides for the "reserved sacrament" with a rubric at the end of the communion service explicitly stating, *"The Sacrament may be reserved in a suitable receptacle for future services."* This rubric lends credence that a doctrine of the real and objective presence of Christ in the consecrated bread and wine was assumed in the 1549 Prayer Book.

From the beginning, no one in England really liked the Communion rite. It was a hodgepodge of liturgical compromise designed to appease people of vastly different theological persuasions, from Zwinglian to

Roman Catholic. The very title of the rite: "The Supper of the Lord, and the Holy Communion, commonly called the Mass" signified how broad a spectrum this Eucharist was intended to placate. Diehard reformers would never want to use the term 'Mass' because it smacked of Roman theology, and committed Catholics abhorred the term 'The Lord's Supper' because to them the Mass was a renewing of the sacrifice of Christ on the cross and not a mere memory of some past meal.

Why did Cranmer issue such a conservative book? There is speculation on whether Cranmer at the time adhered to Lutheran Eucharistic theology, and only later moved toward a more Reformed position. And yet, Cranmer himself denied that he had ever been a Lutheran. When he was on the continent with Martin Bucer and other reformers before he became Archbishop, he embraced Reformed theology. If he was not an outright Zwinglian, he was close to it. Although Cranmer had to keep his views private under Henry VIII – and he even sentenced to death 'heretics' who held the same views as himself – it seems evident that after Henry VIII's death, he was intent on a thorough reform of the church that was more Reformed than Lutheran. His ideal seemed to be a mix of Catholic polity (maintaining bishops, priests and deacons) and Reformed theology, especially regarding the sacraments.

Keep in mind that Cranmer by temperament was an extremely cautious man and someone politically astute at Court during time of King Henry. He is one of the very few persons at Court who did not lose his head to the executioner, since Henry had a way of sentencing to death even some of his most loyal subjects, such as Thomas Cromwell. With all the political intrigue, Cranmer survived. It is likely, therefore, that after the death of King Henry VIII, he initially decided to be cautious in church reform – moving toward a vernacular liturgy that could be accepted by both Catholic and Protestant partisans. Clearly, the 1549 Book did not reflect his reformed views, but it was the start of a process that would eventually lead to another Prayer Book.

Michael Davies, who is an English Roman Catholic, suggests that Cranmer viewed the 1549 book as only one stage in a four-fold process of liturgical reform: "*Stage one* was to have certain portions of the unchanged traditional Mass in the vernacular. *Stage two* was to introduce new material into the old Mass, none of which would be specifically heretical. *Stage three* was to replace the old Mass with an English Communion service, which once more, was not specifically heretical. *Stage four* was to replace this service with a specifically Protestant one."[3]

Davies may well be correct that Cranmer was determined to proceed cautiously and incrementally in introducing his liturgical reforms. Over time it is much easier to move people step by step into a new way of worship than to force them to make giant leaps that are more likely to result in opposition. Any clergy who have introduced new worship to a congregation can appreciate how wise is Cranmer's approach here.

If Cranmer proceeded cautiously in introducing liturgical change to the English people in order not to unduly upset them, he failed. The 1549 Prayer Book was disliked by much of the population, not only in southwest England but around the country. Devout Christians felt that arbitrary changes to worship were being imposed on them from London. The faith and worship that had nurtured and sustained them was now gone and in its place was a worship book that seemed a threat to them as Catholic Christians. Eamon Duffy has written eloquently on this matter in his book *The Stripping of the Altars*. While some Anglicans will take exception to his description of the extent of the opposition to the new Prayer Book, there is no doubt that the transformation of Catholic to Protestant England was a difficult one, and came with an enormous price, both socially and spiritually.

## V. The Debate Between Archbishop Thomas Cranmer and Bishop Stephen Gardiner

After the 1549 Prayer Book was ordered used in all English churches, Bishop Stephen Gardiner (1483 – 1555), while dissatisfied with the book, argued that the Communion rite could be given a Catholic interpretation on both Eucharistic sacrifice and real presence. This infuriated the reformers who demanded a book that was unambiguous in Reformed Eucharistic theology. Bishop Gardiner was arrested but he continued to write and argue that the 1549 Prayer Book could be given a Catholic interpretation. Cranmer responded that he had not intended any such interpretation, and a written debate ensued between Cranmer and Gardiner on the meaning and interpretation of the 1549 Prayer Book. At stake was the issue of whether the Church of England would be much like the Orthodox Churches of the East – Catholic without the Pope – or would it be a Reformed Church, much like the continental Reformed churches, but with a prescribed liturgy and bishops. Three issues stood out.

1. **Does the 1549 *Book of Common Prayer* retain the fundamental doctrine of the Roman Catholic Mass?** Bishop Gardiner, who was a staunch Anglo-Catholic (Catholic without the Pope) argued that the Service of Holy Communion could be interpreted as consistent with the Roman Mass, specifically on the subjects of: a) the sacrifice of the Mass, and b) the real and substantial presence of Christ in the consecrated elements of bread and wine. Cranmer rejected both doctrines and argued instead that Christ's sacrifice for the sins of the world was 'once for all' offered on the cross and could never be repeated or even renewed, and the real presence of Christ is received spiritually in the heart by faith and not corporally in the mouth or stomach.

2. **Does the 1549 *Book of Common Prayer* affirm (or at least allow) belief in the real presence of Christ in the bread and wine of Holy Communion?** For Stephen Gardiner, after the break with Rome under Henry VIII, the Church of England remained Catholic in all facets of its doctrine and worship, including its teaching on the Eucharist. Gardiner argued that it was possible to interpret the 1549 Communion rite as allowing for the doctrine of transubstantiation, that the bread and wine by the action of the priest in the words of consecration become really and substantially the Body and Blood of Christ. Cranmer, to the contrary, believed that the eating of Christ's flesh and drinking his blood was to be interpreted figuratively and not literally. "It is the nature of all sacraments to be figures," he argued in his book on the Lord's Supper. "For figuratively he is in the bread and wine, and spiritually he is in them that worthily eat and drink the bread and wine; but really, carnally, and corporally he is only in heaven, from whence he shall come to judge the quick and the dead."[4]

3. **Can the 1549 *Book of Common Prayer* be interpreted in such a way that it affirms (or at least allows) for a belief in Eucharistic sacrifice?** For Stephen Gardiner, the Mass is a sacrifice renewing the one sacrifice of Christ on the cross which is offered by the priest for the living and the dead, including the remission of sins for the souls in purgatory. For Thomas Cranmer, there is no sacrifice of the Mass because the one sacrifice of Christ once offered can never be repeated or even renewed. The Mass is not a sacrifice but a supper, and consequently the church has no altar to make sacrifice but a table to eat a meal. The only sacrifice in the Lord's Supper is one of praise and thanksgiving for the full, perfect and sufficient sacrifice offered by Christ on the cross for the sins of the whole world.

In the end the English Reformation was about the Eucharist. The primacy of the Bible, justification by faith, indulgences, the role of the Virgin Mary, and the number of sacraments were important, but the controversy always came back to the Mass. The Mass was at the heart of the Catholic system. Challenge the Mass and the entire system collapses. Both Gardiner and Cranmer understood this, which is why the debate between these two scholarly men became so intense. Throughout much of the Edwardian kingship, Gardiner would be in prison, just as Cranmer would be imprisoned and eventually executed under Queen Mary. Compromise was not possible. Too much was at issue in this high-stakes contest. In a powerful treatise written in 1546, Bishop Gardiner wrote with passion about what was at stake:

> And herein the devil utters his sophistry, and makes us forget that is continually done before our eyes, and by impossibility of our carnal imaginations, in things above our capacity, seduce us, and deceive us, in the belief of God's high mysteries, and especially in the mystery of the Sacrament of the altar, whereby to hinder us, and deprive us, of our great comfort and consolation.[5]

The debate between Cranmer and Gardiner was inconclusive because the 1549 Prayer Book was sufficiently ambiguous that it could be interpreted in either a Catholic or Reformed way. Cranmer will settle the debate with the 1552 *Book of Common Prayer*. That book, which puts Reformed doctrine in liturgical form, will move the Church of England in a decisively Protestant direction.

# Questions

1.  *The Book of Common Prayer* was designed as one worship book for the entire Church of England. Every parish and cleric was expected to conform to the new usage. In light of today's pluralistic, multicultural, multigenerational environment, is one worship book with one set of worship services feasible, impractical or untenable? Explain your answer.

2.  Given the polarity between Catholics and Protestants on the Eucharist in the sixteenth century, was it feasible or foolish for Archbishop Cranmer to attempt a Prayer Book that would appeal to both factions? Do you think any Prayer Book could please everyone today?

3.  Today we are in a "live and let live" age in which people can think and believe what they like so long as their actions do not impinge on others. In the sixteenth century people were executed for believing the "wrong things" about the Eucharist or some other point of Christian faith. Do you find it strange that people would be willing to go to prison and even to die for their beliefs? Explain your answer.

# SESSION 3

# THE 1552 BOOK OF
# COMMON PRAYER

*The Holy Eucharist is a commemoration, a representation, an
application of the all-sufficient propitiatory Sacrifice of the Cross. If
his Sacrifice of the Mass have any other propitiatory power or virtue
in it than to commemorate, represent, and apply the merit of the
Sacrifice of the Cross, let him speak plainly what it is... – Bishop John
Bramhall, A Replication to the Bishop of Chalcedon's Survey of the
Vindication of the Church of England from Criminous Schism (1656)*

*Stand thou fast, and stay thy faith... upon the strong rock of God's
Word, written and contained within the Old Testament and the New,
which is able sufficiently to instruct thee in all things needful to thy
salvation, and to the attainment of the kingdom of heaven. – Archbishop
Thomas Cranmer, Confutation of Unwritten Verities (1556)*

The 1549 *Book of Common Prayer* was an unfinished work that sought
to appeal to Catholic traditionalists and Protestant reformers. However,
the book produced much controversy. The Protestant reformers, among
them John Calvin, Heinrich Bullinger, Jan Laski, Martin Bucer and
Peter Martyr, argued that the book did not go far enough in a reformed
direction. Traditionalists said the changes were too severe, though Bishop
Stephen Gardiner was prepared to accept the book by giving it a Catholic
interpretation. There was just enough ambiguity in the book for both sides
to be right.

## I. Archbishop Thomas Cranmer

Archbishop Thomas Cranmer, who had been reticent about sharing
his own theological views, finally broke his silence during the ensuing

debate with Bishop Stephen Gardiner. In 1551, Cranmer published *A Defense of the True and Catholick Doctrine of the Sacrament* in which he laid out a basically Zwinglian or receptionist understanding of both the real presence and Eucharistic sacrifice. Here are a few selections from his treatise that indicate just how strongly Cranmer affirmed the positions of Zwingli and other reformed theologians regarding the Eucharist.

> ...This spiritual meat of Christ's body and blood... is not received in the mouth, and digested in the stomach, (as corporal meats and drinks commonly be,) but it is received with a pure heart, and a sincere faith. And the true eating and drinking of the said body and blood of Christ, is with a constant and lively faith to believe, that Christ gave his body and shed his blood upon the cross for us... And this faith God worketh inwardly in our hearts by his Holy Spirit, and confirmeth the same outwardly to our ears by hearing of his word, and to our senses by eating and drinking of the sacramental bread and wine in his holy Supper.[1]

> ...That bread and wine remain after the words of consecration... This is my body, not denying the bread, but affirming that his body was eaten (meaning spiritually) as the bread was eaten corporally.[2]

> ...The substance of bread and wine do remain, to be received of the faithful people in the blessed sacrament, or Supper of the Lord.[3]

> For they teach, that Christ is in the bread and wine: but we say, according to the truth, that he is in them that worthily eat and drink the bread and wine... They say, that Christ is received in the mouth, and entereth in with the bread and wine: we say, that he is received in the heart, and entereth in by faith.[4]

> For the satisfaction of our sins is not the devotion nor the offering of the priest; but the only host and satisfaction for all the sins of the world is the death of Christ, and the oblation of his body upon the cross, that is to say, the oblation that Christ himself offered once upon the cross, and never but once, nor never none but he.[5]

For if only the death of Christ be the oblation, sacrifice, and price, wherefore our sins be pardoned, then the act of ministration of the priest cannot have the same office. Wherefore it is an abominable blasphemy to give that office or dignity to a priest which pertaineth only to Christ; or to affirm that the Church hath need of any such sacrifice; as who should say, that Christ's sacrifice was not sufficient for the remission of our sins; or else that his sacrifice should hang upon the sacrifice of a priest. But all such priests as pretend to be Christ's successors in making a sacrifice of him, they be his most heinous and horrible adversaries.[6]

...The eating of Christ's flesh and drinking of his blood, is not to be understood simply and plainly, as the words do properly signify, that we do eat and drink him with our mouths; but it is a figurative speech spiritually to be [understood], that we must deeply print and fruitfully believe in our hearts, that this flesh was crucified and his blood shed, for our redemption.[7]

From these passages – and there are many more – there is no doubt that Cranmer was a convinced Zwinglian. Like Zwingli, there was no transformation of the bread and wine into Christ's body and blood, no consecration of the elements, and not even setting them apart for a holy use. The bread and wine were almost extraneous to the act of communion which was spiritual and in no way physical. The communicant received Christ by faith in the heart and not physically in the mouth. Moreover, there was no sacrificial offering by the priest, only a sacrifice of praise and thanksgiving by both priest and worshippers alike.

It is therefore highly unlikely that the 1549 Prayer Book could possibly be the final version that Cranmer had in mind. At best, it was an interim book designed to prepare the English people for further liturgical reforms. So, it should not surprise us that in less than three years Cranmer produced a new and more definitive Prayer Book that reflected Reformed theology in liturgical form.

## II. An Overview of the 1552 Prayer Book

The 1552 *Book of Common Prayer* has fewer manual acts of devotion, limited ceremony, and extensive instructions embedded in the worship services. So, for example, instead of distributing ashes on Ash Wednesday, there is a rather wordy instruction on the need for repentance. Similarly, Palm Sunday and the distribution of palms is abolished as the service focuses exclusively on the passion and death of Christ. All Saints Day is maintained, but All Souls Day and prayers for the dead are abolished, lest there be any hint of purgatory.

> Was the English Reformation a reform or a revolution? A viable argument can be made that the 1549 Prayer Book was a conservative reform, much like Vatican II renewed the Roman Catholic Church. However, the 1552 Prayer Book was more than a mere reform. Although structurally the church retained bishops, priests and deacons, the underlying theology of liturgy and ministry was Reformed, including a new shape to the Communion rite. This was more than reform. It was an overhaul of the existing order.

And yet, for all the emphasis on reformed theology, the book retains the Threefold Order of Ministry of bishops, priests and deacons, declaring in the Preface to the Ordinal that "from the Apostles' time there has been these Orders of Ministers in Christ's Church: Bishops. Priests and Deacons..." Even for Cranmer, Calvin and Zwingli had their limits. The Church of England would go far but not as far as the continental reformers would desire.

Here is an overview of the 1552 Prayer Book with what is included and removed.

1. The Daily Offices of Morning and Evening Prayer include a penitential introduction of Confession and Absolution. The Apostles' Creed is said after the readings of Scripture. A lectionary is provided with the Old Testament read once and the New Testament three times every year. The complete 150 psalms are

recited in order every month, with the exception of some feast days when special lessons and psalms are appointed.

2.  Psalms are included as alternatives to the Gospel canticles in Morning and Evening Prayer.

3.  The scriptural sentences at the beginning of the Eucharist are omitted.

4.  The preparation of the table at the offertory is dropped.

5.  The Eucharistic Prayer is transformed into a communion meal without any real presence of Christ in the bread and wine nor any Eucharistic sacrifice except that of "praise and thanksgiving." The prayer by the priest that changes the elements of bread and wine into Christ's Body and Blood is eliminated with the focus on reception without any consecration. In fact, there is no objective location of the presence of Christ in the elements apart from reception.

6.  The Invocation of the Holy Spirit on the elements, what is known as the epiclesis, is eliminated since it could be thought to allow transubstantiation. In its place, Cranmer had a prayer of preparation: "Hear us, O merciful Father, we beseech thee, and grant that we receiving these thy creatures of bread and wine, according to thy Son our Saviour Jesus Christ's holy institution, in remembrance of his death and passion, may be partakers of his most blessed body and blood."

7.  Cranmer also eliminated the "Memorial" in the 1549 Communion rite: "We …do celebrate and make here before Thy divine Majesty, with these Thy holy gifts, the memorial which Thy Son hath willed to make." Cranmer wanted to leave no doubt that nothing in the service could be interpreted as lending any credence to any kind Eucharistic sacrifice as in the Roman Mass.

8.  The communion bread is real bread rather than a special wafer, and after the communion service the curate is authorized to take what remains of the bread and wine "*for his own use.*"

9.  Adoration of the communion elements (and anything that hinted of it) is prohibited.

10. The sentences for the administration for communion are changed for the bread and wine.

- 1549: "The body of our Lord Jesus Christ which was given for thee, preserve thy body and soul unto everlasting life."
  "The blood of our Lord Jesus Christ which was shed for thee, preserve thy body and soul unto everlasting life."
- 1552: "Take and eat this, in remembrance that Christ died for thee, and feed on him in thy heart by faith, with thanksgiving."
  "Drink this in remembrance that Christ's blood was shed for thee, and be thankful."

11. Ritual gestures by the priest are forbidden with no mention of the bread and wine until communion.

12. The exorcism and chrismation are dropped from the baptismal rite, and chrismation from the confirmation rite.

13. The anointing with oil and the provision for Communion from the reserved sacrament are dropped from the Visitation of the Sick.

14. The burial rite is simplified, the Eucharistic proper for burial is dropped, and almost all petitions for the departed are eliminated to avoid any hint of purgatory.

15. The priest's vestments are reduced to cassock and surplice (a black robe with simple white over-robe). References to the chasuble, the Alb, and the cope, and to candles on the altar are omitted.

16. The use of the word 'altar' is replaced with the word 'table' since the worship service is now a supper rather than a sacrifice.

17. The chalice and paten are eliminated, and only a Bible is given to the newly ordained priest. All references to Eucharistic sacrifice and the consecration of the bread and wine into the Body and Blood of Christ are removed, transforming the role of a priest from a cultic minister who offers sacrifice to a pastor who presides at a meal.

18. The term 'Mass' is eliminated.

## III. A Reformed Revision

The 1552 *Book of Common Prayer* removed any ambiguity about the intent or meaning of the worship services. It would be impossible for a traditionalist to give the book a Catholic interpretation. The book was thoroughly Reformed – Zwinglian theology in liturgical form.

What makes the 1552 Communion rite so significant is that it completely reverses the emphasis of the Roman Catholic Mass. The Mass had the consecration as the pinnacle of the liturgy, with the priest saying the words HOC EST ENIM CORPUS MEUM (This is my Body) and HIC EST ENIM CALIX SANGUINIS MEI... (This is the Chalice of my Blood...). After each consecration, the priest raises the consecrated host and chalice, genuflects before the elements as bells are rung signaling the moment of transubstantiation when bread and wine become Christ's Body and Blood for all to adore. In contrast, the 1552 rite has reception of the bread and wine as the focal point. Reception replaces consecration since there is no change in the substance of the elements – they remain bread and wine. Only as they are received by faith does the recipient receive the Body and Blood of Christ – not physically but spiritually – and not in the mouth but in the heart.

*What Did Cranmer Think He Was Doing?* That is the title of a provocative Grove Liturgical Study written by Bishop Colin Buchanan, one of the foremost liturgists of the Church of England. He argued that the 1552 Communion rite was far more radical than what many Anglicans like to maintain. The rite did not bring consecration and reception together in one action, as if the communicant's faith were a response to the changed elements. Rather it abolished the consecration altogether. After the priest said the proper preface for the season, and then recites what is called "the Prayer of Humble Access," *the rubric says: "Then the priest standing up shall say, as followeth."* There is no mention of a 'consecration' nor are there any manual acts such as touching the bread and wine at the words of institution. In fact, there is no mention of bread and wine at all. The priest simply recites a preparatory prayer for communion immediately followed by reception of the elements which are never referred to as the Body of Christ and the Blood of Christ.

There are no changed elements, only the preparation for reception. The bread and wine, in fact, do not seem very important, except as props that help focus the communicant on the spiritual reception of Christ by faith. Nowhere in the service is the bread and wine separated for a holy use nor is there any requirement that the priest consecrate additional bread and wine if needed, since the bread and wine are not necessary to receiving Christ's spiritual presence. The elements throughout the service remain bread and wine, and nothing more. Thus, the rubric at the end of the Communion rite says: *"And if any of the bread or wine remain, the curate shall have it to his own use."* In other words, the curate can take it home and eat it with Sunday dinner. Bishop Buchanan writes:

> There is no conception of 'consecration' anywhere in the service at all. The only moment is reception… If a point of consecration has to be sought – then it is at reception. Thus, by definition any bread or wine left over is mere bread and wine… If the bread and wine are insufficient, then more can and should be obtained and distributed, but no further instruction about the institution need be given to the recipients. Thus, because there is no original consecration, there can be no supplementary consecration…"[8]

The logic of Bishop Buchanan's argument is undeniable. If there is no consecration of the bread and wine – not even setting apart the elements for holy use – then there is no objective presence of Christ in the elements. There is only reception of the bread and wine received by faith. Thus, there can be no adoration of consecrated wafers, no reservation, no processions, and no Eucharistic devotions that would attach any importance to the bread and wine in and of themselves.

> The 1662 Prayer Book Communion rite will refer to a "Prayer of Consecration" with the priest being required at the words of institution to take and break the bread and lay his hand on every chalice or flagon of wine. Clearly the elements take on an importance in 1662 that they did not have in 1552 or even in the 1559 or 1604 Prayer Books.

The one past practice that Cranmer did retain was kneeling to receive the communion elements. This practice was opposed by Bishop John Hooper (1495 – 1555) and most especially by Scottish reformer John Knox (1514 – 1572). At the last minute, when the book was already at the printer, a Black Rubric was inserted at the end of the Communion Service to make clear that by act of kneeling no adoration was intended of the bread and wine. The theology of the rubric reflects the theology of Huldrych Zwingli who taught that there was no real or essential presence in the bread and wine of the Lord's Supper because Christ's body is in heaven and not on earth. The rubric gives the same rationale for denying the real presence, even as it maintains the practice of kneeling as *"a signification of the humble and grateful acknowledging of the benefits of Christ, given unto the worthy receiver…"* And yet, the rubric declares: *"For concerning the Sacramental bread and wine, they remain still in their very natural substances, and therefore may not be adored, for that were idolatry to be abhorred of all faithful Christians, and as concerning the natural body and blood of our saviour Christ, they are in heaven and not here…"*

Finally, architecture reflects belief as much as words. English parish churches were radically transformed by 1552. The stone altars were removed from churches and replaced by wooden tables, symbolizing that the Lord's Supper was a meal to be eaten, not a sacrifice to be offered. By law, all tables had to be made of wood and moved away from the wall into the middle of the congregation. The rubrics of the 1552 book required that *"the Table having at the Communion time a fare white linen clothe upon it, shall stand in the body of the church, or in the chancel, where Morning Prayer and Evening Prayer is appointed to be said. And the Priest standing at the North End of the Table…."* This is the basis for the North End celebration of the Eucharist which was the normal way for the priest to preside at Communion until the latter part of the nineteenth century. It is still practiced in some churches today.

## IV. An Overview of the Contents

The order of contents of the 1552 book is similar to the 1549 book, with some slight variations. After the Preface, the 1552 book adds an explanation Of Ceremonies: Why Some Be, Abolished And Some Retained. This was in the 1549 book but at the very end. Here it is at the beginning after the Preface. The section clearly takes on greater importance and is included in a prominent place to justify why rites and ceremonies needed to be removed, altered, reformed or kept.

Of Ceremonies was originally written by Archbishop Hermann von Wied of Cologne to justify liturgical change in the Catholic and Lutheran Churches. It explains why liturgical practices that may originally have been well-intended can over time become corrupt or even promote vanity and superstition. A ceremony originally designed to draw people closer to God may end up obscuring the glory of God. Moreover, while some zealous reformers wanted to eliminate all Roman Catholic rituals and ceremonies, the section cautions against that kind of radicalism. Some ceremonies may need to be removed, but most can and should be reformed and not abolished. Here are three passages from Of Ceremonies which are worth pondering:

> And although the keeping or omitting of a ceremony (in itself considered) is but a small thing: yet the willful and contemptuous transgression, and breaking of a common order and discipline, is no small offense before God.

> Let all things be done among you (said St. Paul) in a seemly and due order. The appointment of the order, not to private men: therefore no man ought to take in hand, nor presume to appoint or alter any public or common order in Christ's church, except he be lawfully called and authorized thereunto.

> For we think it is convenient that every country should use such ceremonies, as they shall think best to the setting forth of God's honour and glory, and to the reducing of the people to a most perfect and godly living, with no error or Superstition.

After the Preface and Of Ceremonies comes the Liturgical Calendar and Lectionary followed by Morning and Evening Prayer, the Litany, the Collects, Epistles and Gospels for Sundays and feast days, the Lord's Supper or Holy Communion (the title Mass being abolished), Baptism, Confirmation, Matrimony, the Visitation of the Sick and the Burial of the Dead.

Then comes the Thanksgiving of Women after Childbirth Commonly Called The Churching of Women. This is a change of title from the 1549 book which had the Purification of Women, though the ceremony remains the same. Afterwards comes a Commination Against Sinners which may be used at certain times of the year. This service is basically the same as the First Day of Lent Commonly Called Ash Wednesday service in the 1549 Prayer Book, but there is no reference to Ash Wednesday. It is a service of confession and penance, and nothing more.

## V.  The Ordinal

The Form and Manner for the Ordering of Deacons, Priests and Bishops was not included in the 1549 Prayer Book, but is included here and in every subsequent book. The 1552 Ordinal has been deemed defective by Roman Catholics, partly because in the actual ordination of both priests and bishops, there is no mention of the Order to which the candidate is being ordained. However, the rubrics immediately prior to the ordinations do indicate what is being done. Here are the rubrics and the actual words of ordination by the Bishop or Archbishop.

### Ordination of a Bishop
***Rubric:*** *Then the Archbishop and Bishops present shall lay their hands upon the head of the elected Bishop, the Archbishop saying,*
**Archbishop:** Take the Holy Ghost, and remember that thou stir up the grace of God, which is in thee, by imposition of hands: for God hath not given us the spirit of fear, but of power, and love, and of soberness.

### Ordination of a Priest
***Rubric:*** *When the prayer is done, the Bishop with the Priests present shall lay their hands severally upon the head of everyone that receiveth orders: the receivers humbly kneeling upon their knees, and the Bishop saying:*
**Bishop:** Receive the Holy Ghost: whose sins thou doest forgive, they are forgiven and whose sins thou doest retain, they are retained: and be thou a faithful dispenser of the word of God and of his holy Sacraments. In the name of the Father, and of the Son, and of the Holy Ghost. Amen.

In both services, neither the word 'priest' nor 'bishop' is used in the actual words of ordination. This defect would be corrected in the 1662 Prayer Book. Interestingly, in the ordination rite for a deacon, the word 'deacon' is used in the act of ordination: *"Then the Bishop laying his hands severally upon the head of every one of them, shall say,* "Take thou authority to execute the office of a Deacon in the Church of God committed unto thee: in the name of the father, the son, and the holy ghost. Amen."

Why is there a clear reference to the Order being ordained for a deacon, but none for either a priest or bishop? This is one of the mysteries that confounds liturgical scholars. If Cranmer thought there was no need to mention the Order in the act of laying on of hands, then why is it mentioned for a deacon? Is there a theological reason for the omission in the ordinations of priests and bishops? We do not know. However, in the most recent Roman Catholic ordination rites, the laying on of hands by the bishop is done silently without any words whatsoever.

One of the sharp points of debate between Roman Catholics and Anglicans is whether the Church of England intended to retain the historic episcopate in unbroken succession from the time of the apostles. The debate concluded in 1896 when Pope Leo XIII declared Anglican Orders to be "absolutely null and utterly void." The Pope's case is based on theology rather than continuity: that Anglican theology was defective even if the apostolic order itself was visibly maintained.

Based on the explicit words and declared intention of the Preface to the Ordinal in the 1552 *Book of Common Prayer*, the Church of England did indeed intend to continue the apostolic ministry of bishops, priests and deacons, albeit in a different way and with a different understanding from the Roman Catholic Church. The Preface to the 1552 Ordinal declares:

> It is evident unto all men, diligently reading holy Scripture, and ancient authors, that from the Apostles time there hath been these orders of Ministers in Christ's Church: Bishops, Priests and Deacons: which offices were evermore hath in such reverent estimation, that no man by his own private authority might presume to execute any of them, except he were first called, tried, examined, and known to have such qualities as were requisite of the same; And also by public prayer, with the imposition of hands,

appointed and admitted thereunto. And therefore, to the extent that these orders should be continued, and reverently used, and esteemed in this Church of England; it is requisite, that no man (not being at this present Bishop, Priest, nor Deacon) shall execute any of them, except he be called, tried, examined, and admitted, according to the form hereafter following.

The Ordinal then goes on to give the form and manner for the ordering of deacons, priests and bishops, each with their own service, and articulating the understanding of ministry for each order. While the underlying theology in the ordination services for priests and bishops is pastoral rather than cultic, it is clear that the Orders themselves are being maintained. The late sixteenth century divine Richard Hooker (1554 – 1600) in *The Laws of Ecclesiastical Polity* makes this point forcefully:

> The Ministry of things divine is a function which as God did Himself institute, so neither may men undertake the same but by authority and power given them in lawful manner. …Ministerial power is a mark of separation, because it severeth them that have it from other men, and maketh them a special order consecrated unto the service of the Most High in things wherewith others may not meddle. The difference therefore from other men is in that they are a distinct order. …I may securely therefore conclude that there are at this day in the Church of England no other than the same degrees of ecclesiastical order, namely Bishops, Presbyters, and Deacons, which had their beginning from Christ and His blessed Apostles themselves."[9]

In another passage Hooker stated:

> A thousand five hundred years and upward the Church of Christ hath now continued under the sacred regiment of Bishops. Neither for so long hath Christianity been ever planted in any kingdom throughout the world but with this kind of government alone; which is to have been ordained of God.[10]

Hooker is reflecting the theology of the English reformers. For all their zeal to reform the church, they were careful to maintain the Threefold Order of bishops, priests and deacons. This is what makes the English Reformation different from the continental Reformation which largely abandoned the historic episcopate. The English Church maintained the Order but gave it a different theology, transforming the priest from a cultic figure who offers the unbloody sacrifice of the Mass at the altar to a pastor or elder who preaches the word and administers the sacraments to his parishioners.

> For Roman Catholics reviewing the Anglican Ordinal, the issue is whether the church intended to ordain priests who would offer the holy sacrifice of the Mass. Clearly, the answer is "NO!" The Anglican understanding of priesthood is pastoral rather than cultic, emphasizing word and sacrament as opposed to 'offering Mass' as a sacrifice to remit the sins of the living and the dead. In celebrating the Lord's Supper the Anglican priest does not offer sacrifice to God but represents the people before God pleading the full, perfect and sufficient sacrifice of Christ on the cross.

One of the confusions of the Prayer Book retention of the word 'priest' is that it does not mean what we ordinarily think when we hear the word – one who offers sacrifice as with the Old Testament priests, or who offers 'the unbloody sacrifice of Christ on the altar' as with Roman Catholic priests. In contrast, 'priest' in Anglicanism means presbyter, that is, a teaching elder or pastor. The Ordinal uses biblical images such as messengers, watchmen or sentinels, stewards and shepherds to describe the responsibilities of the priest. Offering sacrifice is a description never used because there is only one sacrifice, full, perfect and sufficient, and that is the sacrifice of Christ on the cross. Christ and Christ alone is our great high priest. There is only one priest and that is Christ who bestows the priesthood on the whole church (1 Pet. 2:9). Priests, or more accurately presbyters, are ordained by the church to serve the church. They have important responsibilities such as teaching, preaching and administering the sacraments, but none of those responsibilities include offering Christ's sacrifice for the remission of sins for the living and the dead.

John Whitgift, before he became Archbishop of Canterbury, responded to the Puritan Thomas Cartwright who objected to the word 'priest' in the Ordinal because in common parlance it meant someone who offers sacrifice rather than a minister of the Gospel. Whitgift replied that at the time of the Reformation the Church of England eliminated any sacrificial meaning to the word 'priest':

> …the very word itself, as it is used in our English tongue, soundeth the word presbyter. As heretofore use hath made it to be taken for a sacrifice, so will use now alter that signification, and make it to be taken for a minister of the gospel. But it is mere vanity to contend for the name when we agree of the thing: the name may be used, and not used, without any great offense.[11]

Whether Whitgift was correct that there was no harm in using the word priest, when in fact, presbyter was meant, is problematic. In the nineteenth century, Anglo-Catholics began to interpret the word priest in a way not meant by previous generations. Richard Hooker understood the danger here, and for this reason he advocated for the use of the word presbyter instead of priest. Like Whitgift, Hooker maintained that when Anglicans use the word priest, they really mean presbyter. Hooker asks, "Seeing then that Sacrifice is now no part of the Church Ministry how should the name of Priesthood be thereunto rightly applied?" He then goes on to say that whether presbyter or priest is used matters not: "Although in truth the word Presbyter doth seem more fit, and in propriety of speech more agreeable than Priest with the drift of the whole Gospel of Jesus Christ."[12]

> The Council of Florence (1439) declared that at ordination to the priesthood, the candidate is to be given both a chalice and a patent as symbols of his office, with the bishop saying, "Receive the power of offering sacrifice in this Church for the living and the dead, in the name of the Father and of the Son and of the Holy Ghost." The 1552 ordination rite for a priest has no such provision. Only the Bible is given to the newly ordained priest, with the bishop saying, "Take thou authority to preach the word of God and to minister the holy Sacraments in this congregation where thou shalt be so appointed." Sacrificial language is completely absent from the charge.

In many ways, the 1552 Prayer Book is a thorough reform of the church's liturgy, except in Cranmer's retention of the word priest. Clearly, it would have been better to eliminate the word and replace it with presbyter. British theologian Andrew Atherstone's assessment of the word is correct that "'priest' still remains a highly ambiguous and contested word under which all manner of incompatible theologies have been smuggled into the Church of England" – and we might add, smuggled into many other churches of the Anglican Communion.[13]

On the real presence of Christ in the bread and wine of Holy Communion, Anglicanism has never been too definitive about the matter. To this day, we have theologians, clergy and lay people who are all over the place on their understanding of the Eucharist – people who stand with Cranmer, Zwingli and the English reformers on the one side, and those who favor Roman Catholic, Orthodox or Lutheran approaches, on the other. The Church of England and the Anglican Communion has never defined the nature of the real presence or Eucharistic sacrifice, except as expounded in the Articles of Religion.

Almost all seventeenth century divines were receptionists of one degree or another, reflecting the views of the sixteenth century reformers. Richard Hooker, for example, has given us the most lucid statement of Anglican Eucharistic theology: "The real presence of Christ's most blessed body and blood is not to be sought for in the sacrament, but in the worthy receiver of the sacrament."[14] In this view, the bread and wine remain unchanged, but through the worthy reception of the sacrament the communicant receives the Body and Blood of Christ. This is an understanding of the Eucharist that Cranmer would approve.

Along the same lines, one of the most respected seventeenth century Anglican divines, John Cosin (1594 – 1672), the Dean of Durham Cathedral, denied any reserved sacrament or real presence of Christ in the elements after the Communion service was ended. For Cosin, like so many others, there could not be a 'real presence' without a 'worthy receiver' of the sacrament. He wrote:

> And we also deny that the elements still retain the nature of Sacraments, when not used according to Divine institution, that is, given by Christ's ministers and received by his people; so that Christ in the consecrated bread ought not, cannot, be kept and preserved to be carried about, because he is present only to the communicants. [15]

John Cosin was a not a radical Protestant. He was, in fact, someone with deep Catholic sympathies, especially in liturgy. And yet, even he, like the sixteenth century English reformers, believed that the remaining bread from the the Communion service could be taken home and eaten at the dinner table, and the remaining wine could be put back in the bottle and used on another occasion. For Cosin, if there was a 'consecration' at all, it ended with the service. The bread became only bread, the wine only wine. Thus, there could be no reserved sacrament because there was nothing to reserve.

## VI. A Reformed Worship Book

The 1552 *Book of Common Prayer* brought the Church of England decisively into the Protestant Reformed camp. It was, in many ways, a magnificent book, which has lasted through the centuries to our own day. However, Cranmer's theology of the Eucharist reflected in the Communion Service was too radical a reform for some in the Church of England, especially with the passage of time.

Dr. Eugene Fairweather, one of Canada's foremost theologians, maintained that the 1552 Prayer Book was the most Protestant book that

Anglicanism ever produced, and that since that time the churches of the Anglican Communion have moved in an increasingly Catholic direction, away from the theology and liturgical practices of 1552. As early as the seventeenth century, Anglicans had realized that Cranmer, for all his genius, had gone too far. Cranmer's rubric that *"if any of the bread and wine remain, the Curate shall have it for his own use"* was changed in the 1662 Prayer Book. The 1662 revisers of the Prayer Book fully realized the implications of what Cranmer was saying in the rubric when they gave it a drastic overhaul, creating a reference to unconsecrated elements left over, and strictly stipulating that in any case even these should reverently be consumed in the church by the priest.

Although the language and much of the liturgical structure of the 1552 Communion rite was retained in the 1662 Prayer Book, by the time of King Charles II a different sacramental world existed. The consecrated bread and wine took on a sanctity that they did not possess in 1552. While few, if any, Anglicans believed in transubstantiation, there was a growing number moving beyond receptionism and recognizing that in some undefined way, the bread and wine consecrated by the priest were integrally connected to the Body and Blood of Christ. The Body and Blood were still received by faith, but the elements themselves took a significance in and of themselves.

Between the 1552 and 1662 Prayer Books, the Church of England would mature and solidify its thinking into what we now know as Anglicanism. If the 1549 and 1662 Prayer Books had been the only Prayer Books of the Church of England, the theological divide between Canterbury and Rome might now be bridged. Pope Leo XIII might never have issued his condemnation of Anglican Orders. However, the 1552 (and one can argue the 1559 and 1604 Prayer Books) resulted in a huge chasm between the churches. A few seventeenth century Anglican divines recognized the issues, and the 1637 Scottish *Book of Common Prayer* was an attempt to address them. The result, however, was bitter division and conflict, and the abolition, at least for a time, of the Church of England.

# Questions

1. What does the Eucharist mean to you?
2. What is your preference in ceremonial? Do you prefer a simple "Low church" service that is plain and simple or a "High Mass" with bells and incense? Explain your answer.
3. Should everyone be able to receive the bread and wine of Holy Communion or only members of the church?

# SESSION 4

# THE 1559, 1604 AND 1637
# PRAYER BOOKS

*I shall for my part never deny but that the Liturgy of the Church of England
may be made better; but I am sure withal it may easily be made worse. –
Archbishop William Laud, The History of the Troubles and Trials of the
Most Reverend Father in God, William Laud (first published 1694)*

*Christ is nearer us, when we behold him with the eyes of faith in Heaven,
then when we seek him in a piece of bread, or in a sacramental box here.
Drive him not away from thee, by wrangling and disputing how he is present
with thee; unnecessary doubts of his presence may induce fearful assurances
of his absence: The best determination of the Real presence is to be sure,
that thou be really present with him, by an ascending faith: Make sure thine
own Real presence, and doubt not his: Thou art not the farther from him, by
his being gone thither before thee. – John Donne, Sermons VII.4.795-804*

The 1552 *Book of Common Prayer* was approved by Parliament in
April 1552. On All Saints Day 1552, Bishop Nicholas Ridley celebrated
Holy Communion at St. Paul's Cathedral, London according to the new
rite. However, the life of this Prayer Book was very brief. On July 6, 1553,
the sickly King Edward VI died and was succeeded by his half-sister
Mary Tudor. She was a devout Roman Catholic completely loyal to the
memory of her mother, Catherine of Aragon, the first wife of Henry VIII.
Upon her accession to the throne, Mary sought to restore England to the
Roman Catholic Church. During her reign, *The Book of Common Prayer*
was banned, Protestant bishops and clergy were arrested and executed or
went into exile, and churches were ordered to reintroduce Roman Catholic
liturgy and architecture. Mary's persecution against Protestants was so
fierce and unrelenting that her detractors called her 'Bloody Mary' because
she executed about 300 'heretics' during her reign.

49

Five Protestant bishops were burned at the stake under Queen Mary: John Hooper, Robert Ferrar, Hugh Latimer, Nicholas Ridley and Thomas Cranmer. Foxe's *Book of Martyrs* provided dramatic accounts of their executions. Latimer and Ridley were executed on October 16, 1555. They were tied back to back at the same stake. Just before the fire was lit, Latimer said to Ridley, "Play the man, Master Ridley; we shall this day light such a candle by God's grace, in England as, I trust, shall never be put out." Five months later Thomas Cranmer suffered the same fate. Imprisoned, alone, and under extreme duress, Cranmer signed a statement recanting his views in the hope of saving his life. However, Queen Mary was determined that the man who had annulled her mother's marriage should die. In a sermon before his execution, he renounced his recantation and affirmed his Protestant views, referring to the Pope as the anti-Christ. When the fire began consuming his body, he put the hand that had signed the recantation into the flames and cried out, "This hand hath offendeth." He died on March 21, 1556.

Mary's attempt to reintroduce Roman Catholicism to England may well have succeeded had she lived another five or ten years, according to British historian Eamon Duffy in his chilling work *Fires of Faith: Catholic England under Mary Tudor*. However, she died from stomach cancer in 1558, and her half-sister Elizabeth, the daughter of Anne Boleyn, ascended to the throne. Elizabeth was a committed Protestant. She quickly reissued a new Prayer Book that combined and revised sections from the 1549 and 1552 books. This third *Book of Common Prayer* was published in 1559.

## I. The 1559 Prayer Book

The 1559 Prayer Book brought back the 1552 Prayer Book with some slight revisions aimed at conciliating those with more Catholic leanings.

1. The Black Rubric which denied any *"real and essential presence"* of Christ in the bread and wine was deleted.
2. The 1552 Sentences of Administration of Communion were prefaced by those of 1549, which allowed for belief in the real presence of Christ in the bread and wine, but received by faith.

Thus, the doctrines of the real presence and receptionism were combined. The new wording read:

- The body of our Lord Jesus Christ which was given for thee, preserve thy body and soul unto everlasting life, and take and eat this, in remembrance that Christ died for thee, and feed on him in thy heart by faith with thanksgiving.
- The blood of our Lord Jesus Christ which was shed for thee, preserve thy body and soul unto everlasting life. And drink this in remembrance that Christ's blood was shed for thee, and be thankful.

3. An Ornaments Rubric (subject to varying interpretations) restored vestments of the 'Second Year of the Reign of King Edward VI.' The meaning of this rubric was unclear and interpretations varied considerably.

4. The prayers against the Pope were removed in an effort at conciliation.

5. In 1561 a new calendar containing more than sixty Black Letter Days of the saints was issued. These Black Letter Days were meant to supplement Red Letter Days that acknowledged New Testament feasts and saints.

6. In 1562 a metrical version of the Psalter with a few hymns and metrical versions of certain Prayer Book texts was authorized for use before and after services and sermons.

7. The Thirty-Nine Articles of Religion was approved by the Convocation of 1563 under the direction of the Archbishop of Canterbury Matthew Parker (1504 – 1575). In 1571 a final version of the Articles was issued. Although the Articles were only included in the 1662 Prayer Book, they are indispensable in interpreting any *Book of Common Prayer*. If we are unclear about the meaning of any liturgy in the Prayer Book, look to the Articles for the key to interpretation.

The 1559 Prayer Book is part of what is termed
"the Elizabethan Settlement" that sought to unite
both Catholics and Protestants by a wide breath of
theological interpretation. However, as theologian
Tim Patrick noted, Elizabeth made "concessions
to the Catholics mostly in matters of form, while
in doctrine she frequently adopted the Protestant
position."[1] Keep in mind that her appointed Archbishop
of Canterbury was Matthew Parker, a Protestant
exile in Geneva during the Marian regime.

## II. Still Cranmer's Book

The question arises whether the 1559 Prayer Book was 'Catholic' enough to withstand scrutiny from Roman Catholics. Could one reasonably interpret its Communion liturgy to affirm a doctrine of the real presence of Christ in the consecrated bread and wine? The answer is doubtful for various reasons.

On the face of it, the Communion Service of 1559 is the same as 1552, so the answer is no. The minister recites the words of institution, followed immediately by the administration of communion. There is no invocation of the Holy Spirit upon the elements, nor is there is an "Amen" at the end of the prayer of preparation, so there is every reason to deny that the prayer itself is one of consecration. The prayer recalling the institution of the Lord's Supper is followed immediately by reception of the bread and wine. It is all one action – the minister recalling Christ's institution of the Supper and the communicants eating the bread and wine. This remains 1552 receptionism. If there is a consecration at all, it is when the communicant receives the bread and wine by faith, and not by any action of the priest.

> Receptionism is the view that during the Eucharist the bread and wine remain unchanged after the recital by the priest of the words of institution, but when the communicants receive the bread and wine, they receive the Body and Blood of Christ spiritually by faith. In the 1559 Communion rite, the recital of the words of institution by the priest is never called 'a prayer of consecration,' nor does the priest have anything to do with the elements of bread and wine before administering them to the communicants.

Again, like 1552, there is no rubric requiring the priest to consecrate additional bread and wine if the amount used in the service is not sufficient to communicate everyone. Clearly, any bread or wine will do – and the words of institution need not be repeated. This practice would be revised in the Canons of 1603. Canon XXI mandated that the words of institution be recited any time additional bread and wine is needed. Receptionism would have its limits.

Although there is no Black Rubric in the 1559 Prayer Book that explicitly denies Christ's natural or essential presence in the bread and wine, one of the rubrics at the end of the Communion Service mandates that *"the bread be such as is usual to be eaten at the table, with other meats."* In other words, regular bread is to be used for communion, and not hosts. The reason for this is *"to take away the superstition… in the bread and wine."* Thus, while there is no Black Rubric, there is still the view of no change in the substance of the bread and wine, and therefore no adoration or worship should be given the elements.

Moreover, the *Second Book of Homilies* (1563) on the worthy reception of the sacrament reiterates Cranmer's position that the real presence of Christ in the Lord's Supper is received spiritually by faith. "It is well known that the meat we seek for in this Supper is spiritual food…and not earthly…so that to think that without faith, we may enjoy the eating and drinking thereof…is but to dream a gross carnal feeding, basely… binding ourselves to the elements and creatures."[2] Whether this is called spiritual real presence or receptionism, does not matter. The bread remains bread and the wine remains wine. It is only as they are received by faith does the communicant receive Christ's Body and Blood.

> The Council of Trent condemned receptionism declaring: "If anyone says that after the consecration is completed, the Body and Blood of our Lord Jesus Christ are not in the admirable sacrament of the Eucharist, but are only *in usu*, while being taken and not before or after; and that in the hosts or consecrated particles which are reserved or which remain after communion, the true body of the Lord does not remain, let him be anathema." – Council of Trent, Thirteenth Session, October 11, 1551, Canon 4.

Finally, the rubric in the 1559 book at the end of the service repeats what was allowed in the 1552 rite, that *"if any of the bread or wine remains, the Curate shall have it to his own use."* In other words, there is no reserved sacrament – the bread and wine in the communion service revert back to ordinary usage. The Curate takes the remainder home for dinner.

## III. Anglican Revisionism

Despite these seeming defects in the 1559 Communion Service, some Anglicans did insist on the doctrine of the real presence and even argued that a Prayer of Consecration is implicit in the service, though not specifically stated. The argument was that both Roman Catholics and Anglicans agreed they received the Body and Blood of Christ, the difference was in the mode of reception.

Richard Hooker (1554 – 1600) sought to combine both real presence and receptionism in one coherent doctrinal understanding of Holy Communion. His oft-quoted words in his *Ecclesiastical Polity* reflect the balance that Anglicanism sought to achieve in the Eucharist: "The real presence of Christ's most blessed body and blood is not therefore to be sought in the sacrament but in the worthy receiver of the sacrament."[3]

Bishop Lancelot Andrewes (1556 – 1626) would make this argument to Cardinal Bellarmine in an exchange of letters. He argued that both Anglicans and Roman Catholics received the Body and Blood of Christ at the Eucharist. The only disagreement was on the mode of presence, either an objective presence in the elements themselves as Roman Catholics taught, or a spiritual presence that is received by faith when taking the bread and wine. In an often-cited passage to Cardinal Bellarmine, Andrewes wrote:

> Christ said, 'This is my Body.' He did not say, 'This is my body in this way.' We are in agreement with you as to the end; the whole controversy is as to the method. As to the 'This is,' we hold firm with faith that it is. As to the 'This is the way' (namely, by the Transubstantiation of the bread into the Body) ... there is no word expressed. And because there is no word, we rightly make it not of faith... We believe no less than you that the presence is real. Concerning the method of the presence, we define nothing rashly... It is perfectly clear that Transubstantiation, which has lately been born in the last four hundred years, never existed in the first four hundred..."[4]

In a series of debates with the Roman Catholic theologian Stephen Harding, Bishop John Jewel (1522 – 1571) defended the 1559 Communion Service as having a 'consecration' in the sense that Cranmer expounded in 1549. Yes, Jewel admitted, reception remains the focal point, but a consecration there was.

Bishop Jewel wrote a book that became the first defense of the Church of England. In his *An Apology of the Church of England*, Jewel admitted that the Church of England had departed from the Roman Catholic theology of the Mass, but insisted that it had not departed from Christ, the apostles and the early church. In other words, Jewel claimed, the Church of England did not have a new-fangled doctrine of the Eucharist, but one that was true and faithful to historic Christianity of the first five centuries.

In response to the charges by Catholics that the Eucharistic practice of the Church of England was a Protestant aberration, Bishop Jewel wrote eloquently in defense of Anglican Eucharistic theology and practice. Here is a sample of his arguments in which he maintained that Anglicans receive a real but spiritual presence in the Eucharist.

In the Lord's Supper there is truly given to the believing the body and blood of the Lord, the flesh of the Son of God, which quickens our souls, the meat that comes from above, the food of immortality, grace, truth, and life; and the Supper to be the communion of the body and blood of Christ, by the partaking whereof we be revived, we be strengthened, and be fed unto immortality, and whereby we are joined, united, and incorporate unto Christ, that we may abide in him, and he in us.

We say that the Eucharist, that is to say the Supper of the Lord, is a Sacrament; that is to wit, an evident token of the body and blood of Christ, wherein is set, as it were, before our eyes, the death of Christ and his resurrection, and what act soever he did while he was in his mortal body: to the end we may give him thanks for his death, and for our deliverance: and that, by the often receiving of this Sacrament, we may daily renew the remembrance of that matter, to the intent that we, being fed with the true body and blood of Christ, may be brought into the hope of resurrection and of everlasting life and may most assuredly believe that the body and blood of Christ doth in like manner feed our souls, as bread and wine doth feed our bodies.

We affirm that bread and wine are holy and heavenly mysteries of the body and blood of Christ, and that by them Christ himself, being the true bread of eternal life, is so presently given unto us as that by faith we verily receive his body and blood. Yet we do not say this as though we thought that the nature and substance of the bread and wine is clearly changed…[5]

About fifty years after Bishop John Jewel's defense of the Church of England, Scottish Bishop William Forbes (1588 – 1634) echoed Jewel, stressing the mystery of the Eucharist in which there was indeed a real but spiritual presence for those who received the bread and wine by faith. Bishop Forbes wrote:

The holy Father... most firmly believed that he who worthily receives these mysteries of the Body and Blood of Christ really and actually receives into himself the Body and Blood of Christ, but in a certain spiritual, miraculous, and imperceptible way... The opinion of those Protestants and others seems to be most safe and most right who think, nay, who most firmly believe, that the Body and Blood of Christ are really and actually and substantially present and taken in the Eucharist, but in a way which the human mind cannot understand and much more beyond the power of man to express, which is known to God alone and is not revealed to us in the Scriptures – a way indeed not by bodily or oral reception, but only by the understanding and merely by faith, but in another way known, as has been said, to God alone, and to be left to his omnipotence.[6]

While academic debates about the nature of the Eucharist ensued throughout the European continent and in England, most lay people were content to attend church and simply receive Holy Communion believing that somehow in some way they were receiving Christ's Body and Blood. They did not fret whether the real presence was physical or spiritual. They simply believed the mystery that in receiving the bread and wine they were partakers of the life of Christ. For most people, that was enough.

Queen Elizabeth I wanted a religion where all her subjects could join together at the same table to receive Holy Communion. She wanted to put away the polemics about the Mass or the Lord's Supper and focus on devotion and piety, believing that in some mysterious and unexplainable way that in receiving the bread and wine she was, in fact, receiving Christ's Body and Blood. Elizabeth is reported to have quoted a verse from the poet John Donne affirming her faith in Christ's presence at Holy Communion:

'Twas God the word that spake it,
He took the bread and break it;
And what the word did make it,
That I believe, and take it.[7]

## IV. The 1604 Book of Common Prayer

On March 24, 1603, King James VI of Scotland became King James I (1566 – 1625) of a united England and Scotland. Almost immediately upon the King's ascendancy to the throne, the Puritans issued a Millenary Petition that requested changes to the Prayer Book. They objected to several practices and usages such as the sign of the cross in Baptism, the use of the surplice, the ring in marriage, the reading of the Apocrypha and Baptism by the laity. Many Puritans also disliked fixed forms of worship and preferred a common order or structure only.

The Hampton Court Conference of 1604, which was presided by King James I, authorized a revision that became the 1604 *Book of Common Prayer.* The book is almost identical to the 1559 Prayer Book, but it did make one concession to the Puritans limiting the ministration of private baptism to authorized ministers, but still allowing the laity to baptize in cases of emergency.

Despite his Presbyterian upbringing in Scotland, King James I moved the Church of England towards greater Catholic ceremonial and solemnity. The early Stuart period saw the moving of the communion table back to the East wall and placed there in such a way that it could be perceived as an altar. Rails were put around it, and though this was defended to keep the dogs from fouling them, it also provided the place where worshippers received communion. The ministers were at the table in the chancel, the people in the nave, and they now had to be summoned to communion. This meant that there was now no continuity between consecration and reception.

King James I was succeeded by his son Charles I (1600 – 1649) who was married to a Roman Catholic. It is not true that Charles was sympathetic to Roman Catholicism. He disliked the Roman Catholic Mass that his wife attended. He also disliked the Catholic priesthood and the idea that priests were separate and different from ordinary Christians. However, the king, like his father, appreciated form and ceremony, believed that church liturgy should be decent and in good order, and that the English king and nation should be independent from all outside authority, spiritual and temporal. Charles was a nationalist who believed in the divine right of kings. In his view there was no room for papal jurisdiction in England.

That said, Charles appreciated ritual, solemnity and reverent worship properly ordered.

## V. William Laud and the 1637 Scottish Book of Common Prayer

Charles I appointed William Laud (1573 – 1645) as Archbishop of Canterbury in 1633. He was the ideal choice to carry out the king's vision for the church. Laud disliked Puritanism, was sympathetic to having images and statues in churches, insisted the communion table be properly adorned (what became known as the Laudian frontal) and generally had a sentimental attraction towards the externals of Catholic worship. He viewed the scriptures and the creeds, as interpreted by the early church, as the foundations of Christian faith. This meant he was more amenable to Catholic faith and practice than the Puritans. He seemed to support doctrines of the real presence, Eucharistic sacrifice, sacramental penance (auricular confession to a priest), ecclesiastical hierarchy and apostolic succession. Puritans were adamantly against these Catholic doctrines. Laud was firmly committed to episcopal order, the divine right of kings and bishops, and disliked any kind of democracy. His was a hierarchical world of top-down command and control. Given a Parliament dominated by Puritans who demanded access to power, his policies were bound to cause controversy.

William Laud could only go so far in imposing his views on the English Church, but he saw his opportunity to impose Catholic order in the 1637 Scottish *Book of Common Prayer*. This was a dangerous move, since the Church of Scotland, though having Anglican bishops, was Presbyterian in sentiment. In concessions to the Scottish Presbyterians, the new book downplayed the Apocrypha, substituted the word "presbyter" for "priest," and used the King James Version rather than the Great Bible for Scriptural passages.

The 1637 Scottish *Book of Common Prayer* is often referred to as 'Laud's Liturgy,' but it was the principal work of Scottish bishops John Maxwell and James Wedderburn. Laud, however, had considerable influence over the book. He and Wedderburn would have preferred to use the 1549

Eucharistic Prayer but they felt they could not go that far in Scotland. Instead they sought to adapt the 1559 Communion Service to the older forms and order of 1549 without overriding the entire structure. They added an *epiclesis* ("vouchsafe so to bless and sanctify with thy Word and Holy Spirit these Thy gifts and creatures of Bread and Wine…"), but other than that, the Communion rite was not all that different from Cranmer's. There was no "Amen" at the end of the Prayer of Consecration so the movement from the words of institution to reception of the elements was the same as with the 1559 book.

Critics charged that by adding an *epiclesis,* the Scottish Communion rite was implying that the bread and wine are changed into Christ's Body and Blood. Laud rejected the claim: "The Corporal Presence of Christ's Body in the Sacrament is to be found in this Service Book." Moreover, he rejected the charge that he believed the Prayer of Consecration implied transubstantiation. The bread and wine "are not transubstantiated in themselves into the Body and Blood of Christ, nor is there any Corporal Presence in or under the elements," he maintained. The bread and wine are only "unto us" the Body and Blood of Christ who take them by faith.[8]

Archbishop Laud believed the 1637 Prayer Book would be a compromise that all factions in Scotland could agree upon. Instead of being accepted, the new book was violently opposed by the Scottish people. It resulted in the Church of Scotland becoming Presbyterian, with a small Anglican remnant remaining as the Episcopal Church in Scotland. Whatever its theological merits, the 1637 Scottish Prayer Book exasperated the already strained relations between Archbishop and Parliament. In 1640, Archbishop Laud was imprisoned, and in 1645, he was beheaded. King Charles I would suffer the same fate in 1649.

We think of Archbishop Laud as having Catholic sympathies, but, as Edward Carpenter, the former Dean of Westminster Abbey has noted, "he entertained deep intellectual convictions which kept him away from Rome. Twice in his lifetime he was approached with an offer of a cardinal's hat if he changed his allegiance; but, as he reported to the King, 'something dwelt within me which would not suffer that, till Rome were other than it is.'"[9] Laud appreciated many things about Catholicism but at heart he was a Protestant who could not accept any infallible authority. He believed Roman Catholicism to be un-English. He supported a national religion, not a universal or international one. He believed there could be many national churches around the world, but no one infallible, authoritative church. And so, an Anglican he remained and an Anglican he died. He would be the fourth Archbishop of Canterbury to suffer a violent death.

With the imprisonments and deaths of Archbishop Laud and King Charles, the Puritans completely controlled England. In 1653 Oliver Cromwell became Lord Protector and ruled England until his death in 1658. Cromwell's son Richard then assumed power but had neither the skills nor the temperament to lead England during these turbulent times. In 1660, the son of the executed king returned to England and ascended the throne as Charles II. Puritanism, however, was not dead. It would rise again in the Glorious Revolution of 1689 with the exile of the autocratic King James II, the calling of William and Mary to reign in England, and the rise of parliamentary power and constitutional monarchy. What Charles I had resisted unto his death came to fruition by the end of the century.

During the Puritan ascendancy to power, the Church of England as it had existed from the time of St. Augustine of Canterbury was abolished by act of Parliament. Bishops were removed from dioceses and many but not all priests from parishes. *The Book of Common Prayer* was made illegal to use in public or private worship. Congregationalist, Presbyterian and Independent ministers dominated the land. The period under Oliver Cromwell saw the Church of England in the wilderness. Some thought it was forever dead, but it came back to life in 1660 with the accession of King Charles II to throne. From the exilic period, the Church of England would solidify its doctrine and liturgy and become a reformed Catholic church that was not Protestant only or Catholic only, but Protestant and Catholic at one and the same time.

# Questions

1. The 1559 Prayer Book is often referred to as the Elizabethan Settlement that sought a middle way between Elizabeth's more Catholic and more Protestant subjects. How do you view the

present Prayer Book – as a compromise or a definitive statement of the church's faith?

2. Some churches have standards of conduct or belief before allowing members to receive Holy Communion. Should the church require standards of belief or behavior on members before they come forth for communion?

3. Should differences in the way Christians understand Holy Communion be a barrier to welcoming people from other churches in receiving the bread and wine?

# SESSION 5

# THE 1662 BOOK OF COMMON PRAYER

*Our Liturgy is an admirable piece of devotion and instruction. It is the marrow and substance of all that the piety and experience of the first five centuries of Christianity found most proper to edification in the public assemblies. It is a compound of texts, of Scripture, of exhortations to repentance, of prayers, hymns, psalms, doxologies, lessons, creeds, and of thanksgivings; of forms for the administration of Sacraments and for other public duties of Christians in the Church; and of commination against impenitent sinners. And all this mixed and diversified with great care expressly to quicken devotion and stir up attention. – The Dean of Windsor and Wolverhampton John Durel, The Liturgy of the Church of England Asserted in a Sermon on I Cor. 11:16 (1662)*

*The Religion of the Church of England, by Law established, is the true Primitive Christianity; in nothing new, unless it be in rejecting all that novelty which hath been brought into the Church. – Bishop Simon Patrick, The Notes of the Church as laid down by Cardinal Bellarmine (1687)*

The 1637 *Book of Common Prayer* precipitated a Scottish rebellion with the result that the Church of Scotland became Presbyterian. Meanwhile in England, church-state relations deteriorated. The English Civil War, really a series of civil wars, lasted roughly from August 22, 1642, to September 3, 1651. During that period, Archbishop William Laud and King Charles I were executed, and Parliament ruled the nation until Oliver Cromwell was appointed Lord Protector of England in 1653. *The Book of Common Prayer* was suppressed in 1645 and the Church of England was outlawed. Bishops were deprived from their dioceses and ordered not to engage in any ministry. Most acquiesced to the new order, though a few bishops did try to minister to clergy and laity surreptitiously. It was a dark time for those Anglicans who yearned for Catholic faith and order in England. As Gilbert Sheldon, who would later become Archbishop of Canterbury lamented, episcopal clergy were persecuted "under a civil authority [which] though not pagan, [was] yet clearly anti-Christian, and such as endeavor to destroy the Church of God."[1]

Oliver Cromwell died in 1558 and was succeeded by his son Richard. He was quite different from his father in personality, temperament and political skills. He was more a Protestant than a Puritan, having neither the passion nor commitment to maintain a semi-theocratic state. It became quickly obvious that Richard lacked the authority to govern a divided Parliament of Puritans, Presbyterians and Royalists. In May 1659 he resigned as Lord Protector and the country plunged into political chaos and economic upheaval. Finally, the army declared the son of Charles I to be the King of England.

When Charles II entered London to cheering crowds on May 29, 1660, he quickly moved to re-establish the old order. In this, he had the law on his side, because "all Acts of Parliament, subsequently passed without the consent of the King were automatically null and void."[2] With the assistance of his Lord Chancellor the Earl of Clarendon, and churchmen such as William Juxon and Gilbert Sheldon, the Church of England was re-established by May 1661. Bishops were either reappointed to their dioceses or consecrated to fill vacant ones. The Bill of Uniformity passed by Parliament declared that no one could minister in a parish church that was not authorized or legally ordained by the bishop of the diocese.

The Savoy Conference held from April to July 1661, was an attempt to reconcile the Puritans with the Church of England. From the beginning, the negotiations proved difficult. The Puritans believed that certain acts required by the Prayer Book were not just misguided but sinful: the sign of the cross at Baptism, wearing the surplice, pronouncing all baptized infants regenerate, the giving of a ring in marriage, and being compelled to kneel in receiving Communion. Anglicans regarded these matters as the right of a national church to ordain ceremonies which are not repugnant to the Word of God. In the end, the conference was unable to agree on any of these issues.

There was one issue, in particular, which Anglicans refused to make any concession: that clergy presently ministering in a parish who had not received episcopal ordination be required to do so. Although Anglicans were not about to de-church their continental Protestant counterparts, they required that their own clergy receive episcopal ordination. There would be no exceptions.

Upon the failure of the Savoy Conference to reconcile Puritans and Anglicans, a committee of bishops began work on revising the 1604 Prayer Book. The revised Prayer Book was passed by the Convocations of Canterbury and York in December 1661 and was approved by Parliament in May 1662. Thus came into existence the 1662 *Book of Common Prayer*.

The 1662 *Book of Common Prayer* is, on the surface, a conservative revision of previous editions. Relatively few changes were actually made from the 1604 Prayer Book. Some occasional prayers, thanksgivings and the "Sea Forms" were added, the Athanasian Creed and the Articles of Religion were included, and a few changes were made in texts among which were the inclusion of a petition for the blessing of baptismal water and a commemoration of the departed. There also was a service of Baptism for those of Riper Years which considered the work of foreign missions and adults converting to Christianity.

## I. The Requirement of Episcopal Ordination

One significant difference from previous Prayer Books is that the ordination rites were tightened against Presbyterian interpretation, with a clear demarcation between bishop and priest, and the names of the Orders clearly stated in the act of ordination. The Preface to the Ordinal declared the intent of the Church of England to maintain the Threefold Order of bishops, priests and deacons, and that no person should function in ordained ministry or execute any of its Functions "except he be called, tried, examined and admitted thereunto, according to the Form hereafter following, or hath had formerly Episcopal Consecration, or Ordination."

The Act of Uniformity and the requirement of episcopal ordination resulted in the removal of about sixteen hundred Puritan ministers from their parishes, either because they refused episcopal ordination or simply could not in conscience abide by the new dictates of the established church on points of doctrine or practice. This was tragic because many highly competent and faithful clergy were forced out of office, including Richard Baxter (who was offered a bishopric but refused it) and theologian

John Owen. It would have been much more feasible (and beneficial) to allow these clergy to remain in their ministries while requiring episcopal ordination for new ordinands. Over time, the matter would have resolved itself.

The historic episcopate is a difficult issue for Anglicans, especially when in full communion or merger discussions with other churches. There are, to be sure, success stories. Anglican churches have merged with non-episcopal churches to form the Church of South India in 1947, the Church of North India in 1970, the Church of Pakistan in 1970, and the Church of Bangladesh in 1974. The Church of England, the Episcopal Church in the United States and the Anglican Church of Canada have entered into full communion with Lutheran churches, and the Episcopal Church in the United States is in full communion with the Moravian Church.

However, there are failures as well where mergers and full communion talks have been derailed by the historic episcopate. A prime example is the failed merger of the Anglican Church of Canada and the United Church of Canada back in the 1970s. A similar failure happened between the Church of England and the Methodists around the same time.

The central issue is whether the episcopate makes the church or the church makes the episcopate. The Church of Rome has always believed that "where there is Peter, there is the church." No Pope, no church. Anglicans have never claimed the same thing about the episcopate – that without bishops there is no church. We have refused to de-church churches without bishops. Moreover, Anglicanism has never said that bishops are of the "esse" of the church – so essential that without them there is no church. While there is a debate within Anglicanism whether bishops are of the "bene esse" (well-being) or "plene esse" (fullness) of the church, either position should allow Anglicanism to accommodate churches without the historic episcopate in some kind of transitional arrangement.

> The laity have a role to play in the ordination of bishops. Why not let lay representatives of the church join, with the consecrating bishops, in laying hands on the ordinand? After all, the priesthood belongs to the whole church, and not to any one Order ( 1 Peter 2:9). The church makes bishops; the bishops do not make the church.

Whatever our ecumenical sensitivities are today, in 1661, with the executions of both King and Archbishop fresh in the minds of many Anglicans, the Church of England was not about to accommodate the Puritans. The commitment was to maintain the historic Threefold Ministry without any exceptions. One example of this is the change in one of the petitions of the Great Litany. The petition in the 1552 Litany prayed for God "to illuminate all Bishops, Pastors and Ministers of the Church with true knowledge and understanding of thy word." The 1662 alteration read "all Bishops, Priests and Deacons." The Church of England wanted no doubt about the Threefold Order of Ministry. Pastors may have served parishes during the Commonwealth period, but with the restoration of the Monarchy they now had to choose either to submit to episcopal ordination or leave.

## II. The Lord's Supper, or Holy Communion

The most important changes in the new Prayer Book were in the rubrics rather than the text, which represented a heightening of Eucharistic doctrine. At the words of consecration, the rubrics instructed the celebrant *"to take the paten into his hands," "break the bread," "lay his hands upon all the bread," "take the cup into his hand,"* and *"lay his hand upon every vessel (be with chalice or flagon) in which there is any wine to be consecrated."* The elements now took on an importance they did not have in 1559, and certainly not in 1552.

The Eucharistic Prayer was given the title "Prayer of Consecration". This was not an instruction or a preparation for reception, as in 1552, but an act of "setting apart" bread and wine to be the efficacious signs of Christ's Body and Blood. An "Amen" was added at the end of the Prayer of Consecration, sealing the division between consecration and reception. A portion of the Eucharistic prayer was to be repeated if additional elements were needed. Consecrated remains from the administration of communion were to be covered, to indicate clearly that they were consecrated. Either at the end of the service or after the service had concluded, the consecrated elements were to be consumed by the communicants rather than being given to the Curate for his own use. The Curate was allowed to take home only bread that was not consecrated.

> Roman Catholic theology taught (and still teaches) that a sacrament can never be undone. Once the bread and wine are consecrated by the priest, they are the Body and Blood of Christ and can never revert to being mere bread and wine again. Beginning with the 1552 Prayer Book, the Church of England disagreed with this position. Once the Communion Service was over, the Curate was free to take the remaining bread and wine home for dinner. However, by 1662 the Church of England changed its position. The Curate was instructed to consume the consecrated elements remaining after the service. The consecrated elements now took on a permanent sacramental character they did not have in prior Prayer Books. Receptionism might still be the accepted doctrine, but the elements themselves now had a special character and remained 'holy' even when not received by the communicant.

There were some concessions to the Puritans. The Prayer of Humble Access came directly after the Preface and before the Eucharistic Prayer to alleviate concerns about realistic language: "Grant us therefore, gracious Lord, so to eat the flesh of thy dear Son Jesus Christ, and to drink his blood…" The Black Rubric also was restored though in a form that denied not *"any real and essential presence"* as in the 1552 book but *"any Corporal Presence of Christ's natural Flesh and Blood."* Kneeling was retained in the Communion Service as a *"signification of our humble and grateful acknowledgment of the benefits of Christ therein given to all worthy Receivers…"* but *"no adoration is intended, or ought to be done, either unto the Sacramental Bread and Wine there bodily received…"* The rubric continues: *"For the Sacramental Bread and Wine remain still in their very natural substances, and therefore may not be adored; (for that were idolatry, to be abhorred of all faithful Christians); and the natural Body and Blood of our Saviour Christ are in Heaven, and not here; it being against the truth of Christ's natural Body to be at one and the same time in more places than one."*

What had changed since 1552? Bishop Colin Buchanan writes: "In wording (and thus in explicit doctrine), the service stands where it stood in 1552. And yet the 'feel' of it is subtly changed. The priest functions 'up there'. The consecration is a priestly event. The consecrated elements have a special character independently of reception. The rite has now moved to a 1549-type liturgy – it has two moments – consecration and reception."[3]

As in the 1549 and 1552 rite, reception is still the climax of the service. However, there also is a consecration – or a setting apart of bread and wine – that did not exist in 1552 but existed in 1549. The 1662 book is mainly 1552 in structure but 1549 in theology. The bread and wine are not just bread and wine. They are, in some sense, set apart and made holy as the Body and Blood of Christ received by faith. Objective presence and personal faith are no longer distinguished from one another but intrinsically linked together. By means of the consecrated bread and wine the communicant receives by faith the Body and Blood of Christ.

An example of the theological shift from 1552 to 1662 is the Catechism included in the 1662 Prayer Book. In addition to sections on the Creeds and Ten Commandments (on which Anglicans and Puritans would agree), there was a section on the Sacraments that reflected the viewpoint of seventeenth century Anglican divines more than the sixteenth century English reformers. Here are some of the key questions and answers:

> **How many Sacraments hath Christ ordained in his Church?**
> Two only, as generally necessary to salvation, that is to say, Baptism, and the Supper of the Lord.
>
> > (This does not exclude the other five "commonly called sacraments" – Confession and Absolution, Confirmation, Matrimony, Ordination and Holy Unction which are not "generally necessary to salvation" and are not specifically appointed by Christ.)
>
> **What meanest thou by the word Sacrament?**
> I mean an outward and visible sign of an inward and spiritual grace given unto us, ordained by Christ himself, as a means whereby we receive the same, and a pledge to assure us thereof.

(This definition teaches that sacraments communicate what they signify. They are not bare ordinances as the Anabaptists and other radical reformers taught, but as Article XXV of the Articles of Religion declares, "certain sure witnesses, and effectual signs of grace, and God's good will towards us.")

**Why was the Sacrament of the Lord's Supper ordained?**
For the continual remembrance of the sacrifice of the death of Christ, and of the benefits we receive thereby.

(The Eucharist is not just a meal but a remembrance of the sacrifice of Christ – the key word being "remembrance" (*anamnesis*) which implies a dynamic, ongoing present reality for worshippers. Article XXVIII of the Articles of Religion characterizes the Lord's Supper as "a Sacrament of our Redemption by Christ's death: insomuch that to such as rightly, worthily, and with faith, receive the same, the Bread which we break is a partaking of the Body of Christ; and likewise the Cup of Blessing is a partaking of the Blood of Christ.")

**What is the inward part, or thing signified in the Supper?**
The Body and Blood of Christ, which are verily and indeed taken and received by the faithful in the Lord's Supper.

(Here is the basis for the Anglican doctrine of the real presence of Christ in receiving the bread and wine by faith in Holy Communion. Again, Article XXVIII declares: "The Body of Christ is given, taken and eaten, in the Supper, only after an heavenly and spiritual manner. And the mean whereby the Body of Christ is received and eaten in the Supper, is Faith.")

The seventeenth century Anglican divines articulated this understanding of the Eucharist in their writings. A theme repeated by all of them is that there is a mystical but sacramental presence of Christ in the bread and wine of Holy Communion.

Archbishop James Ussher (1581 – 1656) preached before the House of Commons:

> Thus in the Lord's Supper the outward thing, which we see with our eyes, is the bread and wine; the inward which we apprehend by faith is the Body and Blood of Christ. ...We acknowledge sacraments to be signs; but bare signs we deny them to be. Seals they are, as well as signs, of the Covenant of Grace. ...The Bread and Wine are not changed in substance from being the same with that which is served at ordinary tables. But in respect of the sacred use whereunto they are consecrated, such a change is made that now they differ as much from common bread and wine, as heaven from earth."[4]

John Cosin (1594 – 1672), the Dean of Durham Cathedral, while he did not believe the presence of Christ continued in the bread and wine after the Communion service was ended, still declared: "For the Body and Blood of Our Savior are not fitly represented by the elements, but also by his institution really offered to all of them, and so eaten by the faithful mystically and sacramentally; whence it is, that He truly is and abides in us, and we in Him."[5]

Archbishop John Bramhall (1594 – 1663), in response to a French Roman Catholic who sought to convince King James I of the real presence of Christ in the Eucharist, wrote that "no genuine son of the Church of England did ever deny the real presence of Christ in the sacrament. Christ said This is My Body; what He said, we do steadfastly believe. He said not, after this or that manner..."[6]

Many Anglicans, of course, had no interest in speculating how or when the bread and wine of Holy Communion became the Body and Blood of Christ. There was, however, a consensus that in the partaking of the bread and wine by faith, communicants were indeed receiving Christ into their lives. The priest had a special role in saying the Prayer of Consecration over the bread and wine, but the Body and Blood of Christ were still received by faith. Nathaniel Eaton (1609 – 1674), for example, was a lay person, scholar and President-Designate of Harvard College, whose poem on the Ascension reflected this new balanced thinking about Communion:

yet it is confesst
That when the holy Elements are blest
By the priest's powerful lips, though nothing there
To outward sense but bread and wine appear,
Yet doth there under those dark forms reside
The Body of the Son of Man that died.[7]

## III.  Lex Orandi, Lex Credendi

One of the historic maxims used by Anglicans and Roman Catholics is *lex orandi, lex credendi* – the law of praying is the law of believing. The phrase dates back to the fifth century theologian Prosper of Aquitaine. How we pray reflects what we believe is one way of interpreting the phrase. Thus, if one wants to know what Anglicans believe, look to our Prayer Book. For Anglicans, doctrine and prayer go together. John Selden, an attorney and Member of Parliament, put it succinctly in a debate with the Puritans when he said: "To know what was generally believed in all ages, the way is to consult the Liturgies, not any man's private writing. As if you would know how the Church of England serves God, go to the Common Prayer Book, consult not this or that man."[8]

Bishop Lancelot Andrewes, in a response to Cardinal Bellarmine, claimed that the faith of the Church of England was contained in a simple formula: "One canon… two testaments, three creeds, four councils, five centuries and the series of the Fathers in that period… determine the boundaries of our faith."[9] The church teaches nothing contrary to the historic faith nor adds anything to it as necessary to salvation.

The Preface to the 1662 Prayer Book makes the point that its underlying theology is not of any particular person or movement or new idea, but the historic faith of the church grounded in Scripture:

…For we are fully persuaded in our judgements (and we here profess it to the world) that the Book as it stood before established by law doth not contain in it anything contrary to the Word of God or to sound doctrine, or which a godly man may not with good conscience use and submit unto, or which is not fairly defensible against any that shall oppose the same…

There is no distinctive Anglican theology in the Prayer Book. While Lutherans have Luther, and Presbyterians have Calvin, and other Reformed churches have Zwingli and Bullinger, Anglicans do not have any one figure who shapes our theology. Even Archbishop Thomas Cranmer, who gave us the 1549 and 1552 Prayer Books, does not have the theological weight that other churches give to their founders and theological leaders.

The Church of England is not a new church founded by a charismatic reformer like Luther or Calvin, but one dating back to the time of the Apostles. King Henry VIII severed jurisdiction with Rome, but the Church in England continued after as before as the Church of England. Over time, the church achieved a reformed Catholicism that eliminated medieval accretions while maintaining Catholic faith and order. It is a church in equilibrium between Catholic heritage and Protestant reform – a church that does not compromise for the sake of expediency but accommodates for the sake of truth. It is a church maintaining what is essential to Catholic faith and order, but being free to discard what has become corrupt or outdated with the passage of time. This is the genius of Anglicanism – not Catholic or Reformed, but Catholic and Reformed at one and the same time.

> For Anglicans, the terms Catholic and Protestant complement rather than conflict with one another. At the time of the Reformation, Anglicans became Protestant in order to become more truly and perfectly Catholic. The Articles of Religion, the Homilies and the Prayer Book are the three constitutive elements of classical Anglicanism. These three, taken together, represent a church that is at one and the same time both Catholic and Reformed.

Anglican divines since the latter part of the sixteenth century have promulgated the view that the Church of England, and by extension Anglicanism around the world, adheres to a reformed Catholicism that is "Catholic" in all the essentials of faith (Scripture, Creeds, Sacraments and Historic Episcopate) but "Protestant" in affirming the truths of the Reformation such as justification by faith and the primacy of Scripture. The intent of the English Reformers was to return to the teachings of

Scripture and the early church without adding anything new to Christian faith or removing anything essential. Theirs was a conservative reformation because it was truly a reform and not a revolution, designed to renew an existing church rather than to remake it.

Perhaps no seventeenth century Anglican divine articulated the position of the Church of England more effectively than Bishop Jeremy Taylor (1613 – 1667). He wrote of the Church of England:

> We have the Word of God, the Faith of the Apostles, the Creeds of the Primitive Church, the Articles of the first four General Councils, a holy Liturgy, excellent prayers, perfect sacraments, faith and repentance, the Ten Commandments and the sermons of Christ, and all the precepts and counsels of the Gospel. We teach the necessity of good works, and require and strictly exact the severity of a holy life. We live in obedience to God, and are ready to die for him, and do so when he requires us so to do. We communicate often. Our priests absolve the penitent. Our bishops ordained priests, and confirm baptized persons, and bless their people and intercede for them. And what could here be wanting for salvation?[10]

By the time of the 1662 Prayer Book, the Church of England began to identify itself as a *'via media'* – the middle way that is at one and the same time both Catholic and Reformed – what some Anglicans refer to as a "reformed Catholicism," or as the evangelical Charles Simeone termed it, "a moderate Calvinism." Catholic faith and order balanced by tempered but Reformed doctrine – that is the great synthesis in Anglicanism.

The 1662 *Book of Common Prayer* remains the official Prayer Book of the Church of England, and its impact on Anglican Churches around the world is enormous. We have in the Prayer Book a spirit that is biblical, liturgical and pastoral. It is a book not just for clergy but for all members of the church. The entire church has both ownership and responsibility for it. The language of the Prayer Book has edified and inspired countless millions over the centuries. Through this book people have come to experience and encounter God in life-changing ways.

No one in Anglicanism has expressed the balance in our doctrine and worship more colorfully than Simon Patrick (1626 – 1707), the Bishop of Ely, who had little liking for either Roman Catholics or radical Protestants. Bishop Patrick put it this way:

> As to Rites and Ceremonies of Divine Worship, they do highly approve that virtuous mediocrity which our Church observes between the meretricious gaudiness of the Church of Rome and the squalid sluttery of the fanatical conventicles. Devotion is so overclad by the Papists that she is oppressed and stifled with the multitudes of her own garments… Some of our modern reformers to make amends have stripped her stark naked, till she is become in a manner cold and dead. The Church of England only hath dressed her as befits an honourable and virtuous matron.[11]

Bishop Patrick's view, though colorfully stated, is true. At the end of the seventeenth century, there was quite a contrast in worship styles throughout Europe. Roman Catholics opted for opulence, ornate architecture, embroidered vestments, inspiring music and beautiful though elaborate ceremonial. This was the Baroque movement in all its grandeur. Continental Protestants had stark churches, in many cases whitewashed and barren of any art, with austere music, long sermons and very little ritual. Services mainly consisted of a pastoral prayer, scripture readings and a sermon with music interspersed. Lutherans sought a middle ground, valuing upfitting architecture and music, as witnessed by Johann Sebastian Bach and other Lutheran composers. Anglicans, much like their Lutheran counterparts, sought a middle way between the ornate and the austere, and nothing better represents this than the architecture of Sir Christopher Wren who designed St. Paul's Cathedral, London. Here was the beauty of holiness and the holiness of beauty that lifted the hearts of worshippers to heaven but focused their minds on word and sacrament.

A nineteenth century Anglican polemicist compared church reform to a thorough housecleaning. Roman Catholics were reluctant to get rid of anything in the house and enjoyed playing with old, dusty and worn-out stuff in the attic. Protestants were so zealous to clean house that they were willing even to throw out the furniture to ensure pristine cleanliness.

Anglicans duly cleaned the house, discarded the old and antiquated but kept what was essential for comfortable living. Whether true or not, many Anglicans thought of their church in those terms. Since the Reformation, the Church of England had undergone a thorough housecleaning while maintaining what is essential.

# Questions

1. Advocates of The 1662 *Book of Common Prayer* claim that it reflects a "reformed Catholicism" – a via media between Roman Catholicism and Protestantism. How do you view your own Prayer Book?
2. In an age that has gone through SARS, the Ebola Virus and now the Coronavirus, do you feel comfortable receiving the wine from a common cup?
3. Is it ever right to use a non-alcoholic drink, such as grape juice, in place of wine for Holy Communion?

# SESSION 6

## WHAT THE REFORMATION WAS ALL ABOUT: EUCHARISTIC PRESENCE AND SACRIFICE

*The sufficiency and perfection of Christ's sacrifice once made upon the Cross and the priesthood in Christ of the whole Church, of which the ordained ministry is representative. The presence of Christ by his gift in the hearts of all who worthily and with faith receive the Holy Communion. – Principles (d) and (f) of the Six Principles of Wycliffe College, Toronto*

*The Roman (Catholic) and Reformed (Calvinistic) really are the only traditions of Christian thought that have range and resources sufficient to become full-scale world-and-life-views – philosophies of life, in the old rich sense of that phrase, seeing all reality, activity and community steadily and whole, because it is all being looked at in relation to God's cosmic goals and plans and to the eternity (the world to come) to which it is all working up. – Dr. J. I. Packer, A Kind of Noah's Ark? The Anglican Commitment to Comprehensiveness (1981)*

In Sessions One through Five we traced the history of *The Book of Common Prayer* from its origins in pre-Reformation England to 1662. What, we might ask, was the great divide between the Church of Rome and the Church of England? An emerging nationalism and the marriage problems of Henry VIII were certainly issues that resulted in England's break with Rome. Justification by faith, indulgences and the primacy of Scripture were all contributing factors dividing Christians one from another. However, at least in regard to the English Reformation, there is one issue that overrides all others: the nature of the Lord's Supper, also called Holy Communion, the Eucharist or the Mass. On this issue, all other issues hinged.

So, before continuing our history of *The Book of Common Prayer*, we should pause and think through the two issues at the heart of the Reformation divide: Eucharistic presence and sacrifice.

# I. The Church Prior to the Reformation

At the Last Supper, when Jesus had shared bread and wine with his disciples as part of the Passover meal, he said to them, "Do this in remembrance of me" (Lk. 22:19, NRSV). Even before any of the Gospel accounts of the Last Supper were written, St. Paul wrote, "The cup of blessing that we bless, is it not a sharing in the blood of Christ? The bread that we break, is it not a sharing in the body of Christ? Because there is one bread, we who are many are one body, for we all partake of the one bread" (1 Cor. 10:16-17, NRSV). The meaning of that ritual in which Christians would gather together, eating bread and drinking wine in memory of Jesus, has been the subject of dispute from the early Middle Ages.

Strangely enough, the early church had few, if any, Eucharistic controversies. There were controversies about the deity of Jesus, the Holy Spirit and Mary the Mother of God, but there was no significant dispute about the meaning of the Lord's Supper. The church was quite content to experience Christ at the Eucharist without trying to define the nature of his presence. St. Justin in the second century and Hippolytus in the third century recount what Eucharistic gatherings might have looked like, but there was no formal liturgy as we understand it today. In fact, according to New Testament scholar P.H. Davids, until about 250 A.D., "when the concepts of priest, sacrifice and altar begin to appear with respect to the Eucharist, the Lord's Supper was a re-enactment of the Last Supper or the fellowship meals of Jesus and his disciples. That is, it was a potluck meal with bread broken at the beginning and a cup of wine shared at the end."[1]

After 250 A.D., sacrificial language becomes more pronounced. With the legalization of Christianity by Constantine and the centralization of Western Christianity under the papacy, the Eucharist takes on a more definitive shape with priests at the altar consecrating bread and wine into the Body and Blood of Christ. The great Eucharistic controversies would begin to appear in the early Middle Ages.

Paschasius Radbertus (785 – 865) was the Abbott of Corbie in France. In 831 he wrote a treatise titled *Concerning Christ's Body and Blood* which asserted that in the Mass the bread and wine become the physical body of Christ that appeared on earth. Christ, Radbertus claimed, can be in many places at once through the Eucharist because God creates anew the flesh and blood of Christ in the consecrated bread and wine. At the Mass, the elements become literally Christ's flesh and blood.

Radbertus wrote his treatise to explain the mystery of the Eucharist to his monks. However, not all of them agreed with him. One of his monks, Ratramnus (died 866) wrote a treatise to refute his Abbott, a work titled *Concerning the Body and Blood of the Lord*. Ratramnus claimed that the Body and Blood of Christ were symbolically or metaphorically present but not literally.

> The view of Radbertus and Ratramnus would lay the groundwork for the two competing views of the Eucharist at the time of the Reformation. One view would affirm the corporal presence of Christ's flesh and blood, while the other would maintain the spiritual presence of Christ, symbolized by the bread and wine, and received by faith.

Two hundred years later, Berengar of Tours (999 – 1088), an accomplished theologian and head of the cathedral School of Saint-Martin, advanced the interpretation of Ratramnus that the bread and wine are the Body and Blood of Christ in a symbolic sense, but not literally. We receive Christ spiritually in our hearts but not physically in our stomachs. Church authorities consistently condemned Berengar for his views, and he was excommunicated by Pope Leo IX. To regain good standing in the Church, Berengar was forced to make the following profession of faith before the Council of Rome in 1079:

> I, Berengar, believe with my heart and confess with my mouth that the bread and wine which are placed upon the altar are the mystery of the sacred prayer and the words of our Redeemer substantially changed into the true and real and life-giving flesh and blood of Jesus Christ our Lord, which was born of the Virgin and which hung on the cross as a sacrifice for the salvation of the world, and which sits at the right hand of the Father, and the true blood of Christ which flowed from his side, and not just by the sign and virtue of the sacrament but in its real nature and true substance…[2]

After his recantation, Berengar retired to ascetic solitude in the priory of Saint-Cosme where he never wrote anything about the Eucharist again. He died in 1088.

Transubstantiation would become the official doctrine of the Roman Catholic Church at the Fourth Lateran Council in 1213. Unlike the belief in the corporal flesh and blood of Christ, transubstantiation is more nuanced, claiming that the bread and wine in their substance or essence become the Body and Blood of Christ, but their accidents – their empirical qualities such as taste, smell, touch and sight – remain unchanged. Transubstantiation was articulated persuasively by Thomas Aquinas (1225 – 1274), though prior to the Reformation there were dissenters who favored the views of Ratramnus and Berengar of Tours, most notably Peter Waldo (1140 – 1205), John Wycliffe (1320 – 1384) and Jan Hus (1372 – 1415).

By far, however, the greatest challenge to transubstantiation came not from a religious reformer but a Franciscan friar. William of Ockham (1287 – 1347) was an English Franciscan friar who is most famously known for 'Ockham's Razor' (also translated from the Latin as 'Occam's Razor') – a methodological principle that bears his name. William argued that only individuals exist, not universals or essences. With no metaphysical universals, the distinction between substance and accident makes no sense. Bread is bread; wine is wine. There is no logic to making them something other than what they are.

The twentieth century philosopher Bertrand Russell, in explaining Ockham's Razor, stated that if one can explain a phenomenon without assuming this or that hypothetical entity, there is no ground for assuming it. One should always opt for an explanation in terms of the fewest possible causes.[3] Ockham himself argued one should not multiply entities beyond necessity. "For nothing ought to be posited without a reason given unless it is self-evident (literally known through itself) or known by experience or proved by the authority of Sacred Scripture."[4]

So how can we understand Christian faith? Ockham espoused fideism, stating that "only faith gives us access to theological truths."[5] In other words, the 'how' of Christianity will ever remain a mystery beyond human reason, but the 'what' is accepted by faith. Applying this to the Eucharist, one can appreciate the reasoning and logic of the reformers. That one receives Christ's Body and Blood is made certain by faith, but whether or how there is any change in the elements is a mystery beyond reason. The 'how' will always be a matter of speculation, but the 'what' is received by faith.

## II. Presence and Sacrifice at the Time of the Reformation

Martin Luther was influenced by the philosophy of William of Ockham. Luther rejected transubstantiation, but he adhered to the real presence of Christ in the Eucharist. How could he affirm Christ's presence but reject transubstantiation? His answer was sacramental union. The bread and wine are Christ's Body and Blood in much the same way that Christ is both divine and human. Although Christ has two natures (deity and humanity), he is one person. So also with the sacrament: it is bread and wine but also the Body and Blood of Christ – physical and spiritual but both integrally linked together. Lutherans would later term this doctrine "consubstantiation" – that Christ is present "in, with and under" the bread and wine of Holy Communion.

Ulrich Zwingli, a more radical reformer than Luther, taught a doctrine of the Eucharist similar to that of Ratramnus and Berengar of Tours. For Zwingli, the Body and Blood of Christ is metaphorical and symbolical only. The bread is a figure or symbol of Christ's Body. The wine is a figure or symbol of Christ's Blood. There is no change of substance, nor is Christ "in, with and under" the bread and wine, as Luther posited. The bread and wine are received by faith, and by faith the communicant receives Christ's Body and Blood – a spiritual but not a corporal communion.

Zwingli and Luther met to resolve their differences on the Lord's Supper at Marburg Castle from October 1 through 4, 1529. The discussions have since become known as the Marburg Colloquy. Zwingli was fond of repeating that Christ's body is in heaven, and therefore he could not be in more than one place at one time. As for Luther's assertion that Christ said: "This is my Body," and "This is my Blood," Zwingli replied that Christ also said, "I am the door" and "I am the gate" and so forth. These are figurative expressions, not literal ones. In the same way, Zwingli argued, the bread is not the literal Body of Christ nor the wine his literal Blood. They are figurative expressions, and it is a disservice to Scripture to interpret them literally. Luther, on the other hand, insisted that when Christ said, "This is my Body," he meant it – the bread was the Body of Christ and not just a symbol. As a result of the disagreement, the Lutheran and Reformed churches would be divided on a central doctrine of Christian faith, thus weakening the Protestant witness against Roman Catholicism.

While the 1549 Prayer Book was more Lutheran than Zwinglian, there is little doubt that the 1552 Prayer Book was Zwingli's Eucharistic theology in liturgical form. At the heart of the 1552 Prayer Book was the Communion rite that radically revised the doctrines of Eucharistic presence and sacrifice.

***Eucharistic Presence***: The 1552 Communion rite rejected the Roman Catholic teaching of transubstantiation that the bread and wine really and substantially become the Body and Blood of Christ – that in their substance or essence, they are no longer bread and wine. Archbishop Cranmer was intent on replacing transubstantiation with a doctrine that would later be termed 'receptionism' – that in receiving the bread and wine by faith, a person receives the Body and Blood of Christ spiritually but not corporally.

Neither Cranmer nor any of the English reformers denied Christ's sacramental presence in the reception of Holy Communion, but they did deny any carnal or corporal presence in the elements of bread and wine. Christ is received spiritually by faith, not in the elements themselves. As Cranmer put it:

> And the bread and wine be not so changed into the flesh and blood of Christ, that they be made one nature, but they remain still distinct in nature, so that the bread in itself is not his flesh, and the wine his blood, but unto them that worthily eat and drink the bread and wine, to them the bread and wine be his flesh and blood; that is to say, by things natural and which they be accustomed unto, they be exalted unto things above nature. For the sacramental bread and wine be not bare and naked figures, but so pithy and effectuous, that whosoever worthily eat them, eateth spiritually Christ's flesh and blood, and hath by them everlasting life.[6]

**Eucharistic Sacrifice**: The other doctrine in the 1552 Prayer Book was the rejection of Eucharistic sacrifice: that at every Mass the priest offers Christ on the altar to remit the sins of the living and the dead. Cranmer was unsparing in his condemnation of this doctrine:

> The greatest blasphemy and injury that can be against Christ, and yet universally used through the popish kingdom, is this, that the priests make their mass a sacrifice propitiatory, to remit the sins as well of themselves as of other, both quick and dead, to whom they list to apply the same. Thus, under pretense of holiness, the papistical priests have taken upon them to be Christ's successors, and to make such an oblation and sacrifice as never creature made but Christ alone, neither he made the same any more times than once, and that was by his death upon the cross.[7]

In the 1552 Communion rite, Cranmer made unmistakably clear the one sacrifice of Christ once offered, can never be repeated or even renewed. In the prayer of preparation before reception of communion, the priest says: "Almighty God, our heavenly father, which of thy tender mercy didst give thine only son Jesus Christ, to suffer death upon the cross for our redemption, who made there (by his one oblation of himself once offered) a full, perfect and sufficient sacrifice, oblation and satisfaction, for the sins of the whole world…" For Cranmer and all the English reformers, the one sacrifice of Christ once offered on the cross was the only sacrifice necessary for every Christian to be right with God. The priest presiding at the communion table was not there to offer sacrifice but to plead the one sacrifice already offered by Christ for the sins of the world.

Cranmer and other reformers based their views of Eucharistic sacrifice on the writings of the New Testament and the early Church Fathers of the first five centuries. The Epistle to the Hebrews was particularly relevant because it seems to exclude any sacrifice other than Christ's once for all sacrifice on the cross (See: Hebrews 4:14-16; 5:7-10; 7:24-25, 27; 9:25-28; 10:1-4, 11-14, 18). The priest pleads the one sacrifice of Christ at Communion but does not repeat it or even renew it. In response to Christ's sacrifice, there is on the part of the congregation a sacrifice of praise (Heb. 13:15). In addition, there is a sacrifice by worshippers offering their "souls and bodies" in response to Christ's offering for them. But there is no distinctly priestly sacrifice in which the one sacrifice of Christ is made present on the altar. In fact, there is no altar, only a communion table to eat a supper, not offer a sacrifice.

On the issue of Eucharistic sacrifice, Cranmer and the other reformers had a strong case that the Mass is not a sacrifice as Roman Catholics understood it. However, the sacrifice of the Mass is at the heart of the Roman Catholic system. If that doctrine was rejected, then there would be no priesthood, no priests, no Masses for the living and the dead, no ability to remit the sins of the souls in purgatory – it would mean the collapse of the Roman Catholic Church. Rome, therefore, felt compelled to respond to the greatest threat to its existence since prior to the Emperor Constantine.

## III.  The Roman Catholic View on Presence and Sacrifice (The Council of Trent)

The twin doctrines of Eucharistic presence and sacrifice have divided Anglicans and Roman Catholics to this day, and resulted in Pope Leo XIII declaring in his Bull *Apostolicae Curae* (1896) that Anglican Orders are "absolutely null and utterly void." To understand Leo's rejection of Anglican Orders, one must first grasp the theology of the Roman Catholic Mass as taught by the Council of Trent which convened between 1545 and 1563.

The Council of Trent was called by Pope Paul III (1468 – 1549) to deal with the Reformation controversy but also to reform the Roman Catholic Church, remove any mistaken impressions or even errors in church teaching, and to articulate the clear and unambiguous doctrine of the Catholic Church in contrast to Protestant churches.

According to the Council of Trent, the Roman Catholic doctrine of the Eucharist consists of the Eucharistic sacrifice, the sacrificial meal, and the sacrificial food – the doctrine of the Mass, of Communion, and of the real presence. The Mass is the renewing of the sacrifice which Christ offered for the atonement of our sins; but the sacrifice also is the sacrament of our union with Christ. The Holy Eucharist is a true sacrament instituted by Christ who is really and substantially present in the consecrated bread and wine even when not being received. The consecrated elements are therefore to be honored and adored. The whole Christ is present in either the consecrated bread or wine, so that it is not essential for the communicant to receive both. The wheat bread and grape wine are transubstantiated by the ordained priest into the flesh and blood of Christ so that only the appearance of bread and wine remains. The sacrament effects union with Christ. It is nourishment for the soul, gives increase in grace and remits venial sin and punishment.

The Canons and Decrees of the Council of Trent, along with the subsequently published Catechism, are quite substantial documents articulating every aspect of Roman Catholic faith. Here are some samples of the Council's teaching on Eucharistic presence and sacrifice.

***Decrees of the Council of Trent, Canon 1 (1551)***: If anyone denies that in the sacrament of the most Holy Eucharist are contained truly, really and substantially the body and blood together with the soul and divinity of Our Lord Jesus Christ, and consequently the whole Christ, but says that He is in it only as in a sign, or figure or force, let him be anathema.[8]

***Decrees of the Council of Trent, Canon 2 (1551)***: If anyone says that in the sacred and holy sacrament of the Eucharist the substance of the bread and wine remains conjointly with the body and blood of our Lord Jesus Christ, and denies that wonderful and singular change of the whole substance of the bread into the body and the whole substance of the wine into the blood, the appearances only of bread and wine remaining, which change the Catholic Church most aptly calls transubstantiation, let him be anathema.[9]

***Decrees of the Council of Trent, Canon 3 (1551):*** If anyone denies that in the venerable sacrament of the Eucharist the whole Christ is contained under each form and under every part of each form when separated, let him be anathema.[10]

***Decrees of the Council of Trent, Canon 4 (1551):*** If anyone shall say that after the consecration is completed, the body and blood of Our Lord Jesus Christ are not in the admirable sacrament of the Eucharist, but are there only in *usu*, while being taken and not before or after, and that in the hosts or consecrated particles which are reserved or which remain after communion, the true body of the Lord does not remain, let him be anathema.[11]

***Decrees of the Council of Trent, Canon 6 (1551)***: If anyone shall say that in the holy sacrament of the Eucharist Christ, the only-begotten Son of God, is not to be adored with the worship of *latria*, also outwardly manifested, and is consequently neither to be venerated with a special solemnity nor to be solemnly borne about in procession according to laudable and universal rite and custom of Holy Church, or is not to be set publicly before the people to be adored and that the adorers thereof are idolaters, let him be anathema.[12]

***Decrees of the Council of Trent, Canon 7 (1551):*** If anyone shall say that it is not lawful that the Holy Eucharist be reserved in a sacred place, but immediately after consecration must necessarily be distributed among those present, or that it is not lawful that it be carried with honour to the sick, let him be anathema.[13]

***Decrees of the Council of Trent, Canon 8 (1551):*** If anyone shall say that Christ received in the Eucharist is received spiritually only and not also sacramentally and really, let him be anathema.[14]

***Decrees of the Council of Trent, Canon 11 (1551):*** If anyone shall say that faith alone is a sufficient preparation for receiving the sacrament of the most Holy Eucharist, let him be anathema.[15]

***Decrees of the Council of Trent, Canon 1 (1562):*** If anyone says that in the mass a true and real sacrifice is not offered to God; or that to be offered is nothing else than that Christ is given to us to eat, let him be anathema.[16]

***Decrees of the Council of Trent, Canon 2 (1562):*** If anyone says that by those words, *Do this for a commemoration me*, Christ did not institute the Apostles priests; or did not ordain that they and other priests should offer his own body and blood, let him be anathema.[17]

***Decrees of the Council of Trent, Canon 3 (1562):*** If anyone shall say that the sacrifice of the Mass is only one of praise and thanksgiving; or that it is a mere commemoration of the sacrifice consummated on the cross but not a propitiatory one; or that it profits only him who receives Communion, and ought not to be offered for the living and the dead, for sins, punishments, satisfactions, and other necessities, let him be anathema.[18]

**Decrees of the Council of Trent, Canon 4 (1562):** If anyone shall say that by the sacrifice of the Mass a blasphemy is cast upon the most holy sacrifice of Christ consummated on the cross, or that the former derogates the latter, let him be anathema.[19]

**Catechism of the Council of Trent (1566):** We therefore confess that the Sacrifice of the Mass is and ought to be considered one and the same Sacrifice as that of the cross, for the victim is one and the same, namely, Christ our Lord, who offered Himself, once only, a bloody Sacrifice on the altar of the cross. The bloody and unbloody victim are not two, but one victim only, whose sacrifice is daily renewed in the Eucharist, in obedience to the command of our Lord: *Do this in commemoration of me.*[20]

**Catechism of the Council of Trent (1566):** …It must be taught without any hesitation that, as the holy Council (of Trent) has also explained, the sacred and holy Sacrifice of the Mass is not a Sacrifice of praise and thanksgiving only, or a mere commemoration of the Sacrifice performed on the cross, but also truly a propitiatory Sacrifice, by which God is appeased and rendered propitious to us.[21]

**Catechism of the Council of Trent (1566):** The Pastor should next teach that such is the efficacy of this Sacrifice that its benefits extend not only to the celebrant and communicants, but to all the faithful, whether living with us on earth, or already numbered with those who are dead in the Lord, but whose sins have not yet been fully expiated.[22]

Both Eucharistic sacrifice and the real presence of Christ in the bread and wine were taught as dogmatic truths by the Council of Trent. At every Mass, the priest renews the sacrifice of Christ on the altar and remits the sins of the living and the dead, including the souls in purgatory. At the act of consecration when the priest says, "This is my Body… This is my Blood…" the bread and wine transform into the Body and Blood of Christ. The 'accidents' remain (taste, touch, smell, shape) but the 'substance' is changed into Christ's Body and Blood – what the church terms 'transubstantiation.' On these two issues, Eucharistic sacrifice and the real presence of Christ in the bread and wine, the Roman Catholic Church has been immovable. It fully and unconditionally stands by these two teachings to the present day.

> On the issue of Eucharistic sacrifice, the Roman
> Catholic Church has tolerated no deviation from
> the decrees of the Council of Trent. Pope John
> Paul II in his many statements on the priesthood
> referred to the priest as an "alter Christus"
> (another Christ) who acts "in personae Christi"
> (in the person of Christ) when celebrating the
> Eucharist. The priest is not a mere representative
> of the faithful but Christ at the altar.

The clearest statement of priestly sacrifice comes from Pope Pius XII's encyclical *Mediator Dei* (1947) in which he wrote: "The fact that the faithful take part in the Eucharistic Sacrifice does not mean that they possess the power of the priesthood. ...the priest acts in the name of the people precisely and only because he represents the person of our Lord Jesus Christ... that the priest, therefore, approaches the altar as Christ's minister, lower than Christ, but higher than the people..." Pope Pius went on to declare:

> The unbloody immolation by which, after the words of consecration have been pronounced, Christ is rendered present on the altar in the state of victim, is performed by the priest alone, and by the priest in so far as he acts in the name of Christ, not in so far as he represents the faithful. But precisely because the priest places the Divine Victim on the altar he presents it as an oblation to God the Father for the glory of the Blessed Trinity and for the benefit of the whole Church.[23]

## IV. Presence and Sacrifice in 16th and 17th Century Anglicanism

The Church of England from the time of Queen Elizabeth I to the 1662 Prayer Book was aware of the teachings of the Council of Trent. Several Anglican divines such as Bishops John Jewel and Lancelot Andrewes engaged in a lively debate with Roman Catholics over the nature of the Eucharist, both on the issues of Eucharistic presence and sacrifice.

While the Church of England had no elaborate confession of faith like many of the continental Protestant churches, it did finalize the **Thirty-nine Articles of Religion** in 1571 to outline or summarize the faith of the church. Here are the key Articles that relate to the Purgatory, the Ordained Ministry and the Eucharist.

1. **Article XXII. Of Purgatory.** The Romish Doctrine concerning Purgatory, Pardons, Worshipping and Adoration as well of Images as of Relics, and also invocation of Saints, is a fond thing vainly invented, and grounded upon no warranty of Scripture, but rather repugnant to the word of God.

   (The doctrine of purgatory is a medieval invention which did not exist before the twelfth century. The idea that one must suffer in the next life before entering into heaven was abhorrent to the reformers and resulted in a system of indulgences that purchased souls out of the pains of purgatory or at least shortened their time in it. Moreover, the reformers rejected any prayer to the saints. We commend them and honor them for their lives, but we pray only to God. As the seventeenth century Anglican divine John Pearson observed concerning the Blessed Virgin Mary: "We cannot bear too reverend a regard for the Mother of Our Lord so long as we give her not that worship which is due unto the Lord himself. Let us keep the language of the Primitive Church. Let her be honored and esteemed, let Him be worshipped and adored."[24])

2. **Article XXIII. Of Ministering in the Congregation.** It is not lawful for any man to take upon him the office of public preaching, or ministering the Sacraments in the Congregation, before he be lawfully called, and sent to execute the same. And those we ought to judge lawfully called and sent, which be chosen and called to this work by men who have public authority given unto them in the Congregation, to call and send Ministers into the Lord's vineyard.

(There is no clear demarcation of bishops, priests and deacons in the New Testament, as Yale Professor David Bartlett has shown in his book *Ministry in the New Testament*. The Threefold Order of Ministry, as it presently exists, is post-biblical and therefore cannot be counted as essential to the church. That is why Anglicans do not "de-church" other Christians, even if we believe that the historic episcopate is of ancient practice and not contrary to Scripture.)

3. **Article XXIV. Of speaking in the Congregation in such tongue as the people understandeth.** It is a vain thing plainly repugnant to the Word of God, and the custom of the Primitive Church, to have public Prayer in the Church, or to minister the Sacraments in a tongue not understanded of the people.

   (There is no evidence in the early church that the Eucharist was ever celebrated in a language other than what the worshipers understood. Since priest and people celebrate the Eucharist together, the language used in the service should be understood by both priest and people.)

4. **Article XXV. Of the Sacraments.** Sacraments ordained of Christ be not only badges or tokens of Christian men's profession, but rather they be certain sure witnesses, and effectual signs of grace, and God's good will towards us, by which he doth work invisibly in us, and doth not only quicken, but also strengthen and confirm our Faith in him.

   There are two Sacraments ordained of Christ our Lord in the Gospel, that is to say, Baptism, and the Supper of the Lord.

   Those five commonly called Sacraments, that is to say, Confirmation, Penance, Orders, Matrimony, and extreme Unction, are not to be counted for Sacraments of the Gospel, being such as have grown partly of the corrupt following of the Apostles, partly are states of life allowed in the Scriptures; but yet have not like nature of sacraments with baptism and the Lord's supper, for that they have not any visible sign or ceremony ordained of God.

The sacraments were not ordained of Christ to be gazed upon, or to be carried about, but that we should duly use them. And in such only as worthily receive the same they have a wholesome effect or operation: but they that receive them unworthily purchase to themselves damnation, as Saint Paul saith.

(The word 'sacrament' is never used in the New Testament, and the first use of the word is by Tertullian around 200 A.D. with reference to baptism. The number of sacraments was constantly debated during the Middle Ages. The Council of Trent formally fixed the number at seven, while most reformers put it at two, Baptism and the Lord's Supper. Anglicans did not completely exclude the other five, but referred to them as "commonly called" sacraments. The phrase is ambiguous and can mean "also called" or "popularly called" or "falsely called." To this day, Anglicans have never resolved the issue. Perhaps the wisest words on the matter came from the seventeenth century divine Edward Gee, the Dean of Lincoln who wrote: "Though we reject those five additional sacraments of the Church of Rome, yet we do it not because they are not sacraments at all. They are not Christ's sacraments, since he never appointed them. This is why we reject the five additional sacraments, since neither the Church of Rome herself, nor all the churches of the world together, are able to institute one sacrament..."[25])

5.  **Article XXVIII. Of the Lord's Supper.** The Supper of the Lord is not only a sign of the love that Christians ought to have among themselves one to another; but rather it is a Sacrament of our Redemption by Christ's death: insomuch that to such as rightly, worthily, and with faith, receive the same, the Bread which we break is a partaking of the Body of Christ; and likewise the Cup of Blessing is a partaking of the Blood of Christ.

    Transubstantiation (or the change of the substance of Bread and Wine) in the Supper of the Lord, cannot be proved by holy Writ; but it is repugnant to the plain words of Scripture, overthroweth the nature of a Sacrament, and hath given occasion to many superstitions.

The Body of Christ is given, taken, and eaten, in the Supper, only after an heavenly and spiritual manner. And the mean whereby the Body of Christ is received and eaten in the Supper is Faith.

The Sacrament of the Lord's Supper was not by Christ's ordinance reserved, carried about, lifted up, or worshipped.

(How the Last Supper and the Lord's Supper are connected is a matter of speculation. St. Paul in I Corinthians 11 tells us that the Lord's Supper is a remembrance of the death of Christ until he comes again. The bread we eat is a partaking of the Body of Christ and the wine we drink is a partaking of the Blood of Christ. Paul never assumes that the bread and wine are anything but bread and wine, even though by eating and drinking them we partake of Christ's Body and Blood. At the same time, the bread and wine are not to be carried about in processions or worshipped in and of themselves, but to be received by faith. The efficacy of the sacrament is in the reception of the bread wine, not in their adoration. We eat the bread and drink the wine but we do not worship them.)

6. **Article XXIX. Of the Wicked which eat not the Body of Christ in the use of the Lord's Supper.** The Wicked and such as be void of a lively faith, although they do carnally and visibly press with their teeth (as Saint Augustine saith) the Sacrament of the Body and Blood of Christ, yet in no wise are they partakers of Christ: but rather, to their condemnation, do eat and drink the sign or Sacrament of so great a thing.

(This article reiterates the spiritual understanding of the Eucharist. Only those who eat the bread and drink the wine by faith receive the Body and Blood of Christ.)

7.  **Article XXX. Of both kinds.** The Cup of the Lord is not to be denied to the Lay-people: for both the parts of the Lord's Sacrament, by Christ's ordinance and commandment, ought to be ministered to all Christian men alike.

    (Hygiene may have been a significant factor in giving the laity only the bread and not the wine, especially after the Black Death ravaged Europe. It also may be true that a strong distinction between priest and laity resulted in the priest only receiving the cup. However, the Council of Trent did affirm that in receiving either the bread or the wine, the communicant receives the full Christ. Still, Anglicans felt it was important that the laity and priest together received the bread and wine since together they are celebrating the Eucharist.)

8.  **Article XXXI. Of the one Oblation of Christ finished upon the Cross.** The Offering of Christ once made is that perfect redemption, propitiation, and satisfaction, for all the sins of the whole world, both original and actual; and there is none other satisfaction for sin but that alone. Wherefore the sacrifice of masses, in which it was commonly said that the Priest did offer Christ for the quick and the dead, to have remission of pain and guilt, were blasphemous fables, and dangerous deceits.

    (In Roman Catholic teaching, at every Mass the priest plays the part of Christ (in personae Christi), the bread and wine are the sacrifice of Christ's Body and Blood, and the communion table is an altar on which the sacrifice is made. Article XXXI rejects this view. The sacrifice of Christ was made once for all upon the cross, and is full, perfect, and sufficient for the sins of the whole world. It cannot be renewed or repeated, nor can a priest offer it to God on our behalf. Christ's once for all sacrifice makes any other sacrifice unnecessary.)

9.  **Article XXXII. Of the Marriage of Priests.** Bishops, Priests and Deacons, are not commanded by God's Law, either to vow

the estate of single life, or to abstain from marriage: therefore it is lawful for them, as for all other Christian men, to marry at their own discretion, as they shall judge the same to serve better to godliness.

(The First Lateran Council in 1123 made celibacy mandatory for priests, although it took hundreds of years to fully implement. The reformers saw no reason for this requirement, since some of the apostles, including St. Peter, were married. Anglicans chose to go back to the practice of the early church and allow clergy to marry.)

10. **Article XXXVI. Of Consecration of Bishops and Ministers.** The Book of Consecration of Archbishops and Bishops, and Ordering of Priests and Deacons, lately set forth in the time of Edward the Sixth, and confirmed at the same time by authority of Parliament, doth contain all things necessary to such Consecration and Ordering: neither hath it anything, that of itself, is superstitious and ungodly. And therefore whosoever are consecrated or ordered according to the Rites of that Book, since the second year of the forenamed King Edward unto this time, or hereafter shall be consecrated or ordered according to the same Rites; we decree all such to be rightly, orderly, and lawfully consecrated and ordered.

(The Ordinal of the Church of England revised the Roman Catholic understanding of priesthood. In Roman Catholicism, priests are ordained to offer sacrifice on the altar during the celebration of Mass. In Anglicanism, priests are called to be pastors and teachers. Anglican clergy are not 'Mass-priests' but presbyters or teaching elders who preach the word and celebrate the sacraments. The Anglican priesthood is primarily a pastoral ministry that nurtures and cares for the people, teaching them to love God and neighbor, and to care for others.)

By 1662, the Church of England had experienced controversies and upheavals from the Puritans, and continued criticism from Roman Catholics. After the Restoration of the Monarchy under Charles II, the church had the opportunity to revise its Prayer Book and respond to the criticisms made against it. Although there were some significant changes in the rubrics – the celebrant needed to consume rather than take home for dinner the remaining consecrated bread, was required to say the words of institution if additional bread and wine were needed for communion, and the Communion Prayer itself became a "Prayer of Consecration" with an "Amen" at the end of it – the Prayer Book itself remained remarkably similar to previous books. One significant addition was the inclusion of the Black Rubric, which was in the 1552 book, and then removed in 1559. That rubric was a concession to Puritans about the meaning of kneeling for communion. The final version read:

> *Whereas it is ordained in this Office for the Administration of the Lords Supper, that the Communicants should receive the same Kneeling; (which Order is well meant, for the signification of our humble and grateful acknowledgement of the benefits of Christ therein given to all worthy Receivers, and for the avoiding of such profanation and disorder in the holy Communion, as might otherwise ensue). Yet, lest the same Kneeling should by any persons, either out of ignorance or infirmity, or out of malice and obstinacy, be misconstrued and depraved; It is hereby declared, that thereby no Adoration is intended, or ought to be done, either unto the Sacramental bread or wine, there bodily received, or unto any Corporal Presence of Christ's natural Flesh and Blood. For the Sacramental bread and wine remain still in their very Natural Substances, and therefore may not be adored, (for that were Idolatry, to be abhorred of all faithful Christians). And the natural body and blood of our Saviour Christ are in Heaven, and not here; it being against the truth of Christs Natural body, to be at one time in more places than one.*

Anglican preachers from the seventeenth century to present times have emphasized a real but spiritual presence – not a corporal presence or transubstantiation, but a real presence, nonetheless. We may not receive

Christ with our mouths but we do receive him into our hearts. No one has better preached on the real presence than John Donne, Dean of St. Paul's Cathedral in the early seventeenth century. He assured his congregation:

> When thou come to this seal of thy peace, the Sacrament, pray that God will give thee that light, that may direct and establish thee, in necessary and fundamental things; that is, the light of faith to see, that the Body and Blood of Christ, is applied to thee, in that action; But for the manner, how the Body and Blood of Christ is there, wait his leisure, if he have not manifested that to thee: Grieve not at that, wonder not at that, press not for that; for he hath not manifested that, not the way, not the manner of his presence in the Sacrament, to the Church.[26]

There was a general view in Anglicanism that by means of the bread and wine, the communicant by faith received the Body and Blood of Christ. The mode of presence, or exactly how this should be, was left undefined. Anglicans were content to term this a mystery, while Roman Catholics felt compelled to define it by reliance on Aristotle's categories of substance and accident, interpreted by St. Thomas Aquinas and other medieval scholastics. Mystery versus definition – this was the divide on the real presence after 1662.

On Eucharistic sacrifice, there was more variation. Cranmer in his *Defence of the True and Catholick Doctrine of the Sacrament* is unflinching in his attack on the Sacrifice of the Mass and the power of the priest to offer such sacrifice. The only sacrifice Cranmer is willing to acknowledge is one of "laud, praise, and thanksgiving," but he specifically excludes any "sacrifice propitiatory." He rejected any notion of a sacrificing priest:

> For if only the death of Christ be the oblation, sacrifice, and price, wherefore our sins be pardoned, then the act of ministration of the priest cannot have the same office. Wherefore it is an abominable blasphemy to give that office or dignity to a priest which pertaineth only to Christ; or to affirm that the Church hath need of any such sacrifice; as who would say, that Christ's sacrifice were not

sufficient for the remission of our sins; or else that his sacrifice should hang upon the sacrifice of a priest.[27]

Not only did Cranmer reject a sacrificial priesthood, but he seemed also to say there was no difference between a priest and a layperson, except in the ministration of the office. For Cranmer, the priest does not act 'in personae Christi' nor is the priest an 'alter Christus' as in Roman Catholicism. The priest is, in fact, a functionary, and nothing more, and he stated this in very clear terms in his treatise:

> Therefore Christ made no difference between the priest and the layman, that the priest should make oblation and sacrifice of Christ for the layman, and eat the Lord's Supper from him alone, and distribute and apply it as him liketh. Christ made no such difference; but the difference that is between the priest and the layman in this matter is only in the ministration; that the priest as a common minister of the Church, doth minister and distribute the Lord's Supper unto other, and other receive it at his hands.[28]

Cranmer clearly had no use for the 'holy sacrifice of the Mass' and consistent with his Zwinglian views, believed that the Eucharist was not a sacrifice to be offered but a meal to be eaten. In gathering together for the Lord's Supper, Christians give thanks for the benefits received by Christ's death on the cross, testify that they are members of Christ's body, and eat his flesh and drink his blood spiritually by faith.

And yet, several seventeenth century Anglican divines did not fully accept Cranmer's view, or at least modified it, the most notable being Archbishop William Laud. He wrote:

> At and in the Eucharist we offer up to God three sacrifices: one by the priest only; that is the commemorative sacrifice of Christ's death, represented in bread broken and wine poured out. Another by the priest and people jointly; and that is the sacrifice of praise and thanksgiving… The third, by every particular man for himself only: and that is the sacrifice of every man's soul and body.[29]

Other divines, to one degree or another, shared Laud's view, among them Richard Field (1561 – 1616), the Dean of Gloucester; Francis White (1564 – 1638), the Bishop of Ely; Jeremy Taylor (1613 – 1667), the Bishop of Down, Connor, and Dromore, and several others.

On Eucharistic sacrifice, Anglicans in the seventeenth century were not of one mind on the issue, except to insist that the one sacrifice of Christ on the cross could never be repeated. A few Anglicans felt comfortable terming the Eucharist "a memorial of our redemption." However, most Anglicans would not even go that far. They feared such language would be used to argue for a renewal of the one sacrifice of Christ on the cross, transforming the priest from a representative of the congregation to an "alter Christus" who made Christ's sacrifice present by acting 'in personae Christi.' In Anglicanism, a priest is not Christ at the altar but a representative of the people before God. The priest does not offer sacrifice but pleads the one sacrifice of Christ as the people's representative.

## Questions

1. How, if at all, do you connect the death of Christ on the cross with the Sacrament of Holy Communion?
2. When you receive the communion elements of bread and wine, how do you think you receive Christ: in your mouth and stomach or in your heart by faith? Or both?
3. Lord's Supper, Holy Communion, Eucharist or Mass – which of these terms best describes your understanding of receiving the bread and wine of Christ's Body and Blood?

# SESSION 7

# EUCHARISTIC PRESENCE AND SACRIFICE IN ECUMENICAL DIALOGUE

*Now if anyone asks me how (de modo), I will not be ashamed to admit that the mystery (arcanum) is too sublime for my intelligence to grasp or my words to declare: to speak more plainly, I experience rather than understand it. Here, then, without any arguing, I embrace the truth of God in which I may safely rest content. Christ proclaims that his flesh is the food, his blood is the drink, of my soul. I offer him my soul to be fed with such food. In his sacred supper he bids me take, eat, and drink his body and blood under the symbols of bread and wine: I have no doubt that he truly proffers them and that I receive them. – John Calvin, The Institutes of the Christian Religion, 4.17.32 (1559)*

*At the level of spiritual experience apodictic judgments of nullity and invalidity do not really make sense. In the presence of God's grace and God's power each one is unique and there is no room for a priori assumptions that grace is not operative or less operative because someone does not minister within a set of criteria set down by the Catholic Church. Rather we are drawn to praise what God accomplishes through imperfect instruments whether Catholic, Anglican, or Protestant. – Fr. Jean-Marc Laporte, S.J., A Spiritual Assessment of Anglican and Protestant Orders: Absolutely Null and Utterly Void? (December 10, 2012)*

Despite worship similarities, Anglicans and Roman Catholics seemed far apart in their understandings of both the real presence and Eucharistic sacrifice. However, in the nineteenth century things began to change. The Oxford Movement moved the Church of England to a more Catholic understanding of itself. There also developed a general feeling among many churches that the time had come for Christians to put aside their differences, work together in common mission, and strive for a common faith leading to Christian unity.

# I. Apostolicae Curae and Saepius Officio

At the end of the nineteenth century, several Anglicans sought reconciliation with Rome, the first step being the recognition of the validity of Anglican Orders. There was no question that Anglicans intended to maintain and preserve the Orders of bishop, priest and deacon because that was stated in the Ordinal of 1552 and every Ordinal subsequently. Nor was there any real issue on the line of episcopal succession. It had not been broken or interrupted, as had been the case in the Lutheran Church of Denmark. Anglicans had the historic episcopacy and intended to maintain it, but Rome looked to other matters besides linear succession.

Based on an extensive review of the Prayer Books of 1552, 1559, 1604 and 1662, Pope Leo XIII issued an apostolic letter on September 13, 1896, titled *Apostolicae Curae* in which he declared that "ordinations carried out according to the Anglican rite" are "absolutely null and utterly void" based on defects of form and invalid intention. The Pope maintained that it is essential for the validity of priestly and episcopal ordinations that the bishop's hands should be associated with the words indicating either the order being conferred or else its distinctive grace and power which, for the priesthood, is said to be chiefly that of consecrating and offering the Eucharist. (In 1947 Pope Pius XII ruled that there must be mention of the Order in the act of ordination.) As previously indicated, Anglican ordination rites for a bishop or priest did not mention the specific Order in the act of laying on of hands until the 1662 Prayer Book.

> *Apostolicae Curae* finds the essence of the priesthood in the power to consecrate and offer the Eucharist, and faults the English Ordinals for not specifying this. There is no doubt that the Anglican understanding of priestly ministry is pastoral rather than cultic in that the priest does not offer sacrifice at the altar but instead presides at a meal at a table. The Anglican Ordinals never mention the priest renewing the sacrifice of Christ or offering sacrifice for the living and the dead, because that is simply not Anglican theology. There is a sacrifice of "praise and thanksgiving" but in no way does the priest repeat, re-enact or even renew Christ's one sacrifice once offered on the cross.

While Anglo-Catholics were deeply disappointed by Pope Leo's decision, evangelical Anglicans were not surprised. Although both churches use the word 'priest,' the word has varied meanings. Anglicans are not ordained as 'mass priests' as Roman Catholic clergy are. That has never been the intention of the Church of England or any church of the Anglican Communion. Roman Catholics and Anglican evangelicals understand this better than Anglo-Catholics, as theologian Gerald Bray pointed out:

> We may be grateful to the pope for his clarity on this point, because the claims of high church Anglicans about the supposed 'catholicity' of Anglican orders are false, and rejected by the papacy with good reason. We do not want our clergy to be mass-priests, and are glad they are not officially recognized as such by those who are in a position to know what they are.[1]

The Archbishops of Canterbury and York replied to the Pope's letter with an encyclical titled, *Saepius Officio* which defended Anglican ordinations as maintaining the historic ministry of the church. However, the explanation of Eucharistic sacrifice in Anglicanism is less than persuasive. The bishops stress the sacrifice of praise and thanksgiving, but do not adequately deal with the sacrifice offered by the priest alone. The Archbishops declared in Section XI:

> Further, we truly teach the doctrine of Eucharistic sacrifice and do not believe it to be a 'nude commemoration of the Sacrifice of the Cross'... But we think it sufficient that in the Liturgy which we use in celebrating the holy Eucharist, – while lifting up our hearts to the Lord, and when now consecrating the gifts already offered that they may become to us, the Body and Blood of our Lord Jesus Christ, – to signify the sacrifice which is offered at that point of the service in such terms as these. We continue a perpetual memory of the precious death of Christ, who is our Advocate with the Father and the propitiation for our sins, according to His precept, until His coming again. For first we offer the sacrifice of praise and thanksgiving; then we plead and represent before the Father the sacrifice of the cross, and by it we confidently entreat

remission of sins and all other benefits of the Lord's Passion for all the whole Church; and lastly we offer the sacrifice of ourselves to the Creator of all things which we have already signified by the oblations of His creatures. This whole action, in which the people have necessarily to take its part with the Priest, we are accustomed to call the Eucharistic sacrifice.

Relations with Rome hit a low point in 1896 with the publication of *Apostolicae Curae.* However, the ecumenical movement was renewed with a new spirit of openness in the Roman Catholic Church after Vatican II. Both Anglicans and Roman Catholics hoped that the churches could move beyond the polemics of the past and set forth a common understanding of the Eucharist, the ordained ministry and authority. Thus in 1967 began ARCIC, the Anglican – Roman Catholic International Commission established by the Archbishop of Canterbury Michael Ramsey and Pope Paul VI.

By 1971, the Commission declared that there was "substantial agreement on the doctrine of the eucharist," while acknowledging "a variety of theological approaches within both our communions." The truth is that members of neither church were satisfied with the result. Evangelical Anglicans and traditionalist Roman Catholics were dissatisfied with the Commission's explanations of the real presence and Eucharistic sacrifice. The language used in the Commission's Report was sufficiently vague, ambiguous, and subject to a variety of interpretations that it was difficult to pin down exactly what was being agreed upon.

The Commission was asked to do rethink its report, and in 1979 it published an Elucidation that attempted to respond to the criticisms of the original report. The Elucidation attempted to balance the two competing views prevalent at the time of the Reformation: the transformation of the elements into the Body and Blood of Christ with communicants feeding upon them in their hearts by faith. Again, however, members of neither church were fully satisfied with the result, though some Anglican churches approved the report.

On the issues of the priesthood and Eucharistic sacrifice, the Commission appealed to the Greek word *anamnesis*, often translated as memorial, or memory, or remembrance. The sacrifice of Christ was not repeated, the Commission emphasized, but it was made present through the action of the priest reciting the words of institution in celebrating the Eucharist. The passage in the Report on the Ministry is Paragraph 13:

> The priestly sacrifice of Jesus was unique, as is also his continuing High Priesthood. Despite the fact that in the New Testament ministers are never called 'priests' (*hiereis*) Christians came to see the priestly role of Christ reflected in these ministers and used priestly terms in describing them. Because the eucharist is the memorial of the sacrifice of Christ, the action of the presiding minister in reciting again the words of Christ at the Last Supper and distributing to the assembly the holy gifts is seen to stand in a sacramental relation to what Christ himself did in offering his own sacrifice. So our two traditions commonly used priestly terms in speaking about the ordained ministry. Such language does not imply any negation of the once-for-all sacrifice of Christ by any addition or repetition.

ARCIC was a hopeful sign that relations between the Anglican Communion and the Roman Catholic Church would improve, and there was a genuine optimism that the judgment of *Apostolicae Curae* could be reversed. However, Rome never approved any of the ARCIC reports. On June 29, 1998, the Prefect of the Congregation for the Doctrine of the Faith, Cardinal Joseph Ratzinger (who would become Pope Benedict XVI) issued a *Doctrinal Commentary on the Concluding Formula of the Professio fidei* in which he used Pope Leo XIII's declaration on Anglican Orders as an example of a truth which must be definitively held but is not divinely revealed. This meant that Rome continued to view Anglican Orders as invalid. So, there remains a huge divide between the churches today, with the gap becoming even wider with the ordination of women as both bishops and priests, as well as sexual and gender issues.

> ARCIC attempted to bridge the divide on the Eucharist
> between an objective presence of Christ and the
> personal faith of the believer. Why not have both, ARCIC
> maintained – a real objective presence but received by
> faith? Then what is the point of worshipping the sacrament
> (or host) in Benediction or some other rite of Eucharistic
> adoration without receiving it? How can the sacrament
> stand apart from the faith of the communicant? Both
> Roman Catholic traditionalists and Anglican evangelicals
> saw the same issue. One must either accept that the
> bread and wine are transubstantiated into Christ's Body
> and Blood, an objective presence apart from the faith of
> the communicant, or one must maintain that by means
> of the bread and wine Christ is received by faith, and
> apart from faithful reception there is no real presence.

## II. Contemporary Anglican Thinking on the Eucharist

At this point, Rome does not recognize Anglican Orders. If an Episcopal or Anglican priest wants to become a Roman Catholic priest, that person must be ordained – not re-ordained or conditionally ordained, but ordained as if he never was a priest. The same is true of Anglican bishops, the most famous being Graham Leonard, the former Bishop of London, who converted to Roman Catholicism and was ordained a priest. From "My Lord Bishop" he became "Father Leonard." Anglicans may have the Threefold Order of Ministry in form, but according to Rome they do not have it in substance. They are defective because of their theology on the real presence and Eucharistic sacrifice.

Anglicanism, on the other hand, is generally content to describe both real presence and sacrifice as areas of mystery which ultimately defy definition. Many of our Eucharistic hymns reflect this sense of mystery. A hymn included in both the Canadian and American hymnals is Canon G.H. Bourne's *Lord enthroned in heavenly splendor*. The second verse is a thoroughly Anglican understanding of the Eucharist:

Here our humblest homage pay we,
here in loving reverence bow;
here for faith's discernment pray we,
lest we fail to know thee now.
Alleluia! Alleluia!
Thou art here, we ask not how.[2]

Roman Catholics will often laugh at Canon Bourne's last line of that stanza: "Thou art here, we ask now how." Yet, this is the genius of Anglicanism which is reluctant to define anything too dogmatically that goes beyond the first five centuries of Christian history. Since the number of sacraments had been a matter of debate throughout the Middle Ages, Anglicans have been content to say there are two sacraments – Baptism and the Lord's Supper. These are the sacraments of the Gospel necessary to salvation. The other five "commonly called" sacraments are neither Gospel mandates nor necessary to salvation. Similarly, the mode of Christ's presence in the Eucharist was never mentioned in the New Testament or dogmatically defined by the early church, so why is it necessary to now define it? Anglicans would prefer to live with the mystery and simply say that in every Eucharist there is an encounter with Christ.

> Intentional ambiguity is very much an Anglican theological trait. Where there is no necessity to define, Anglicans do not define, especially where the church of the first five centuries has not declared on the issue. On the real presence of Christ in the bread and wine of Holy Communion, for example, Anglicans are hesitant to define what is, in the end, a mystery. Anglicans believe in the "what" (reception of Christ's Body and Blood by faith) without defining the 'how' (how does it happen?). This is intentional ambiguity: to leave doubtful things doubtful, and live with mystery rather than define and dogmatize.

On the issue of Eucharistic sacrifice, no Anglican would want to say that the priest offers 'the holy sacrifice of the Mass' for the living and the dead, including the remission of sins for the souls in purgatory. Even the notion of 'renewing' or 're-presenting' the sacrifice of Christ on the altar would make most Anglicans cringe. Back in 1563, the Dean of St. Paul's Cathedral, Alexander Nowell, published his Catechism, which is a hallmark of Anglican doctrine. To the question on whether the priest offers Christ's body in sacrifice to God the Father for sins, Nowell wrote:

> It is not so offered. For he, when he did institute his supper, commanded us to eat his body, not to offer it. As for the prerogative of offering for sins, it pertaineth to Christ alone, as to him which is the eternal Priest; which also when he died upon the cross, once made that only and everlasting sacrifice for our salvation, and fully performed the same forever. For us there is nothing left to do, but to take the use and benefit of that eternal sacrifice bequeathed us by the Lord himself, which we chiefly do in the Lord's Supper.[3]

Nowell's Catechism is important because it is considered one of the most thorough elucidations of Anglican doctrine, expanding on the Articles of Religion and the Prayer Book catechism. Dean Nowell reflected what was universally held by leaders of the Church of England in the sixteenth and seventeenth centuries: the one sacrifice of Christ, once offered, full, perfect and sufficient for the sins of the whole world.

Christ's sacrifice on the cross cannot be repeated, renewed or re-presented, but at the Eucharist the priest pleads that one sacrifice on behalf of the congregation. To give two examples from our hymnody, the first from Canon William Bright, a well-known nineteenth century priest and hymnwriter of the Church of England:

> And now, O Father, mindful of the love
> That brought us, once for all, on Calvary's Tree,
> And having with us him that pleads above,
> We here present, we here spread forth to thee
> That only offering perfect in thine eyes,
> The one true, pure, immortal Sacrifice.[4]

Bright wrote his hymn in 1874. Evangelicals were not happy with the hymn because they thought it could be interpreted in a way that the one sacrifice of Christ is made present by the priest celebrating Communion.

In 1889, Bishop E.H. Bickersteth wrote a hymn to correct any misinterpretation in Bright's hymn which became a standard Eucharistic hymn for evangelicals:

> O Holy Father, who in tender love
> Didst give thine only Son for us to die,
> That while he pleads at thy right hand above,
> We in One Spirit now with faith draw nigh,
> And as we eat this Bread and drink this Wine,
> Plead his once offered Sacrifice Divine.[5]

What is significant about these two hymns is that they are not that different. Both plead the once sacrifice of Christ once offered on the cross, and neither claims to represent or even renew that sacrifice. On behalf of the people, the priest pleads Christ's sacrifice, and in heaven Christ pleads for us before the Father. His sacrifice is perfect and sufficient. None other is required. None other can be made.

Lastly, it would be well to keep in mind that even the Episcopal Church in the United States whose churches tend to have more ceremonial than typical Roman Catholic churches, maintains classical Anglican Eucharistic theology. Although there are Roman Catholics who sometimes go to Anglo-Catholic churches to attend 'High Mass,' the theology underlying such a Mass is Anglican and not Roman Catholic – what might be termed reformed Catholicism. The Catechism of the Episcopal Church in the 1979 *Book of Common Prayer* reflects the classical faith of the church on the Eucharist. Although written in contemporary language, and more nuanced than the polemical statements of the past, a seventeenth century Anglican, or even a sixteenth century English Reformer, would still find much to embrace.

> **What is the Holy Eucharist?** The Holy Eucharist is the sacrament commanded by Christ for the continual remembrance of his life, death, and resurrection, until his coming again.

> **Why is the Eucharist called a sacrifice?** Because the Eucharist, the Church's sacrifice of praise and thanksgiving, is the way by

which the sacrifice of Christ is made present, and in which he unites us to his one offering of himself.

**By what other names is this service known?** The Holy Eucharist is called the Lord's Supper, and Holy Communion; it is also known as the Divine Liturgy, the Mass, and the Great Offering.

**What is the outward and visible sign in the Eucharist?** The outward and visible sign in the Eucharist is bread and wine, given and received according to Christ's command.

**What is the inward and spiritual grace given in the Eucharist?** The inward and spiritual grace in the Holy Communion is the Body and Blood of Christ given to his people, and received by faith.

While the answers may seem more nuanced than the language of sixteenth century documents, the catechism is careful to affirm that the church's sacrifice is one of praise and thanksgiving, and there is no reference to any other sacrifice offered by either priest or people. Most Anglicans would say that the priest pleads the one sacrifice of Christ on behalf of the congregation and that communicants receive the benefits by faith.

In his *Catechism*, Alexander Nowell, asked the question: For what use is the Lord's Supper? Nowell answered: "To celebrate and retain continually a thankful remembrance of the Lord's death, and of that most singular benefit which we have received thereby; and that as in baptism we were once born again, so with the Lord's Supper we be always fed and sustained to spiritual and everlasting life."[6]

Although there is over a four hundred year difference between the publication of Nowell's *Catechism* and the 1979 Prayer Book, the teachings of the two books on the Eucharist are almost identical. The 1979 Prayer Book catechism may call the Lord's Supper a 'Mass,' but there is nothing in either the Prayer Book or the catechism that comes close to the sacrifice of the Mass as Roman Catholics understand it. Episcopalians receive the benefits of Christ's sacrifice once offered on the cross, but do not repeat or renew it. Despite appearing to break with the Reformation, the 1979

Episcopal Prayer Book is still thoroughly Anglican with links to Cranmer and the reformers in Eucharistic theology.

## Questions

1. As Christians of differing churches dialogue with each other about the meaning of the Eucharist, do you think we should strive for consensus by using ambiguous language that both sides can agree upon, or should we seek to understand the classical statements of faith upon which our understanding of the Eucharist is grounded?
2. Does participation in Holy Communion bring us God's forgiveness or only remind us that we have already been forgiven?
3. How do you view the Eucharist: as a fellowship meal or as a celebration of the death and resurrection of Jesus?

# SESSION 8

# THE AMERICAN AND
# CANADIAN PRAYER BOOKS

*Such a complete life is pictured in the Church's year. It has its Advent,
Nativity, Epiphany, Lent, Easter, Whitsunday, Trinity Sunday. It fills the
year with its increasing, slowly maturing beauty. This is the true meaning
of the year, with all its sacred seasons. Let us be true Churchmen, and
give it all its richness. Only, dear friends, we do not really honor the
venerable beauty of the Church's calendar when we make it a badge
of our denominational distinction, or deck its seasons out with all the
trickery of colored altar-cloths, purple and white and green, but when
we see in it the story of a human life slowly ripening from God's first
purpose to the full-grown, glorified manhood standing before God's
presence and setting forth God's power to its fellow men. – Phillips
Brooks, Bishop of Massachusetts, Sermon on the First Sunday of Lent*

*Let us come to Christ's Communion Table and celebrate our union
with Him and with one another, putting all fear and selfishness aside,
and praying Him to show us there how rich a thing it is to believe in
Him and how sweet a thing it is to serve Him by His Holy Spirit. –
Phillips Brooks, Bishop of Massachusetts, A Whitsunday Sermon*

As people from England, Scotland, Wales and Ireland flocked to the
North American colonies, *The Book of Common Prayer* came with them.
The 1604 book was the basis for the first service of Holy Communion
in Jamestown, Virginia, in the year 1607. The Rev. Robert Hunt was the
celebrant.

The 1662 Prayer Book was in use at the time of the American
Revolution. After the War of Independence, the Church of England in
the American colonies became the Protestant Episcopal Church in the
United States of America with a new Constitution and *Book of Common
Prayer*. The Prayer Book was authorized at the General Convention of
1789. While the book reflected the spirit of the American Revolution,

its Preface declared that "this Church is far from intending to depart from the Church of England in any essential point of doctrine, discipline or worship." Still, there was intense debate about the proposed Prayer Book led by two prominent members of the church – Samuel Seabury of Connecticut and William White of Pennsylvania.

## I. Samuel Seabury and William White

Samuel Seabury was born in Connecticut. During the Revolutionary War he served as a Chaplain in the British Army. After the war, Seabury decided to remain in America where he was a prominent member of the Connecticut clergy. He was chosen to become the first American bishop, but the Church of England was unable to consecrate him because of legal restrictions. However, the Episcopal Church of Scotland was a "free" church in that it was not established by law (the established Church of Scotland was Presbyterian) and therefore could accommodate Seabury. The Scottish bishops consecrated Seabury in Aberdeen, Scotland with the proviso that the American Episcopal Church agree to use the 1764 Scottish service of Holy Communion, a rite which was similar to the 1549 Communion service.

Seabury was an unlikely person to be chosen the Episcopal Church's first bishop. As a Loyalist during the American Revolution, his sympathies were for aristocracy and hierarchy in both civil and church government. He believed that all authority from God was top-down and not bottom-up. He distrusted ordinary folk in decision-making and he opposed the laity having an equal voice in the church with bishops and clergy. While even the English had moved past the divine right of kings, Seabury still believed in the divine right of bishops. He was adamant that there should be no check on their authority.

William White was Rector of Christ Church, Philadelphia. He would eventually become the first Bishop of Pennsylvania and the third Presiding Bishop of the Episcopal Church. White was a man of the Enlightenment who valued reason and democracy as much as faith and order. His book: *Case of the Episcopal Churches in the United States Considered* begins by asserting "the inherent right of the community to resist and effectually to exclude unconstitutional and oppressive claims."[1] This is an American Anglicanism quite different from its English counterpart, an Anglicanism that reflects both a revolutionary spirit and the Age of Enlightenment.

White maintained that Anglican "faith and worship are rational and Scriptural."[2] The ordering of the two terms is critical. Reason was determinative. If a Scriptural point was deemed reasonable, it was to be accepted; if not, it held no claim to a Christian's allegiance.

Rational faith led to a democratic spirit. For White, authority in the church originated from below with the basic unit of the church being the parish, not the diocese. Moreover, relationships within the church were contractual. Parishes were in a contractual relationship with the diocese, and clergy were in a contractual relationship with their parishes. There was mutual responsibility and accountability on all parties. Historian Ross Hebb has summarized White's view of church polity this way: "Given White's approach, three specific characteristics of the emergent church's polity become apparent. First, the new polity was thoroughly democratic; secondly, authority within the church clearly originated from below; finally, relationships between various bodies within the church were purely contractual."[4]

> William White believed that the parish, not the diocese, was the basic unit of the church, and for this reason there would always be a tension between a democratic spirit and episcopal structure. Ecclesiastical hierarchy there would be, but it would never be absolute and unchecked. Bishops would have standing committees just as rectors had vestries. A century before Lord Acton made his famous statement that power corrupts and absolute power corrupts absolutely, White believed much the same thing.

White further believed "that the episcopate is a part of apostolic ordering of the church, not part of apostolic doctrine."[3] He was prepared to accept episcopacy as the *bene esse* of the church, but he adamantly rejected the notion that it was of the *esse* of the church. He believed it was possible to be valid and legitimate church without episcopacy. White was prepared to accept a Presbyterian form of church government if the English bishops remained prohibited from consecrating American clergy as bishops. Episcopacy might be a good thing but in no way was it essential to the church's existence.

Seabury, in contrast to White, was resolutely committed to the historic episcopate. He believed the church was a divine institution whose authority was from Christ himself. He wrote: "In short, the rights of the Christian Church arise not from nature or compact, but from the institution of Christ; and we ought not to alter them, but to receive and maintain them, as the holy Apostles had left them."[5] Authority, for Seabury, is from above, not below; revelation, not nature or compact, was the cement which held the church together. The Christian religion was revealed in Scripture; there was an objective givenness, a deposit of faith that could not be changed. Seabury maintained that "the government, sacraments, faith and doctrines of the church are fixed and settled. We have a right to examine what they are, but we must take them as they are."[6] In short, Seabury believed that continuity of doctrinal content was the prerequisite of catholic polity.

Here then, was the clash between two competing ecclesiastical views: Seabury's divine right of bishops and the fixed nature of divine religion versus the democratic spirit and contractual relationships advocated by White. The two men could not be farther apart on their vision for the Episcopal Church.

## II. The Proposed 1786 Prayer Book

When the proposed 1786 Prayer Book was being debated, Seabury and White were at loggerheads with one another. Seabury wanted some minor changes in the English Prayer Book and a fuller Prayer of Consecration requested by the Scottish bishops, but White wanted something quite different – a book that would appeal to the Enlightenment mentality of the day. William Smith, a White protégé, wrote that "we live in a liberal and enlightened age." Therefore, "nothing can be considered deserving the name of religion, which is not rational, solid, serious, charitable, and worthy of the nature and perfections of God to receive, and of free and reasonable creatures to perform."[7]

Smith argued that the new Prayer Book should shorten the services of Morning Prayer and the Great Litany to make them more palatable for "the lukewarm and negligent." The Lord's Prayer should be said only once at the Communion Service and all repetition should be avoided. The Psalter should be reworked for greater accuracy and all offensive passages of Scripture should not be used either in the Eucharistic or Daily Office Lectionaries. The concern was that certain Scripture lessons were "inexpedient to read in mixed assemblies" including passages on sex, violence and human unreasonableness. All "hurtful" portions of Scripture were to be avoided.

In addition, both Smith and White proposed that the Athanasian Creed be left out of the book. The Convention agreed and omitted it entirely. Apart from the Preface, the Nicene Creed was also omitted in the proposed 1786 book. Only the Apostles' Creed was included, yet even here there was intense debate on the question of Christ's descent into hell – should that line be removed? Finally, the Articles of Religion was revised with some of them being omitted.

While Connecticut (Seabury's diocese) opposed many of the proposed changes, other deputations wanted further revisions. Virginia suggested eliminating all usage of the Apocrypha. South Carolina wanted changes in the Apostles' Creed and the omission of the Magnificat and Nunc Dimittis. The forces of rational reform wanted a Prayer Book like no other.

## III.  The 1789 American Book of Common Prayer

In 1789, the new American *Book of Common Prayer* was officially ratified. The Preface of the book claimed that "this Church is far from intending to depart from the Church of England in any essential point of doctrine, discipline, or worship." However, the book had some significant differences from the 1662 Book.

- The Prayer of Consecration in the 1764 Prayer Book of the Scottish Episcopal Church was used in place of the one in the 1662 English Prayer Book.
- At the baptism, the marking of the newly baptized child with the sign of the cross was made optional.
- The Articles of Religion was not included in the book.

- The Nicene Creed was reintroduced into the Communion Service, but it was to be chosen only if the Apostles' Creed was not used.
- The Athanasian Creed was not restored.
- The Magnificat and Nunc Dimittis were removed from Evening Prayer. They would be restored in the 1892 Prayer Book.
- The last four verses of Psalm 95 in Morning Prayer were removed and only the first four verses of the Benedictus were retained.
- The three causes for which Matrimony was ordained were removed in the Marriage Service, including the primary purpose of marriage for the procreation of children.
- A new ordination service for priests was introduced.

By the standards of the day, the 1789 Prayer Book was a decidedly latitudinarian worship book in which the compilers felt free to pick and choose what to retain, what to abandon, and what to revise. The 1662 Prayer Book was their guide, but only a guide. The compilers did not feel obliged to make only necessary or cosmetic changes, such as to remove all references to the King and Parliament. Apart from the Communion Service and the elimination of the Articles of Religion, the American book was thoroughly Protestant – a word that was not shunned by American Episcopalians, since they named their church: The Protestant Episcopal Church of the United States of America – PECUSA.

Since 1789, the American Episcopal Church has had three other Prayer Books:

- The Prayer Book of 1892 provided more flexibility within the services of Morning and Evening Prayer, along with enrichment through the study of worship in the Bible and other historical documents.
- The 1928 Prayer Book was designed to offer clearer language, an expanded calendar and a lectionary that eliminated offensive and disturbing biblical passages, as well as a new translation of the 150 Psalms.
- The 1979 Prayer Book was the most innovative of any Prayer Book in Anglicanism when adopted. It included worship services and prayers in both Rite I traditional language and

Rite II contemporary language. It also reflected the liturgical developments of Vatican II and the Liturgical Movement in the Anglican Communion. The longest prayer book ever composed by any church in the Anglican Communion, it contained a large selection of prayers and services, including Noon Day Prayer, Compline, the Reconciliation of a Penitent, several Eucharistic Prayers in traditional and contemporary language, a two-year Daily Office lectionary and a three-year Eucharistic lectionary.

A new Prayer Book is on the horizon in the Episcopal Church. It is sure to stretch the boundaries of what is deemed acceptable in Anglicanism. In many ways, the book will reflect the spirit of William White, Enlightenment and post-modern thinking, moving beyond ecclesiastical restraint and placing a premium on reason and experience in interpreting scripture and tradition.

## IV. The Canadian Prayer Books

The 1662 *Book of Common Prayer* was the liturgy of Canadian Anglicanism, used by every Bishop and Priest from the time of Canada's first Bishop, Charles Inglis (1734 – 1816) in the late eighteenth century, right up to the 1962 Prayer Book. Use of the 1662 Prayer Book reflected more than loyalty to England. It was, as Ross Hebb says in his study of *Samuel Seabury and Charles Inglis*, "the Church's chief repository of doctrine and the primary statement of its view of Scripture, as well as the official and only approved form of worship in the Church of England at home and overseas."[8]

One of the major differences between the American and Canadian Churches is leadership. The four most important leaders of the newly formed Episcopal Church were all born in America: Samuel Seabury of Connecticut, John Henry Hobart of New York, William White of Pennsylvania and Thomas Clagget of Maryland. Americans elected Americans as their bishops, and thus a unique American spirit took hold in the church. In stark contrast, all the major bishops in Canada were British-born and trained: Charles Inglis, Jacob Mountain, John Strachan, John

Medley, Francis Fulford, and others. The Church in Canada held firmly to its British roots while the American Church felt free to go its own way.

> The Anglican Church of Canada continues to have a very hierarchical form of church government with a top-down command and control leadership model. Unlike the Episcopal Church, there are no standing committees in Canadian dioceses to offer advice and consent, or to hold a bishop accountable for his or her actions. There are no checks and balances, since the bishop, is, in effect, the diocese.

The Canadian Church used the 1662 *Book of Common Prayer* throughout the eighteenth and nineteenth centuries. When the church gained autonomy from the Church of England and became "The Church of England in Canada," the Canadian bishops issued a Solemn Declaration in 1893 which is printed at the beginning of the 1962 Prayer Book. Among other things, the declaration states:

> And we are determined by the help of God to hold and maintain the Doctrine, Sacraments, and Discipline of Christ as the Lord hath commanded in his Holy Word, and as the Church of England hath received and set forth the same in *The Book of Common Prayer* and the Administration of the Sacraments and other Rites and Ceremonies of the Church according to the use of the Church of England; together with the Psalter or Psalms of David…and the Forms and Manner of Making, Ordaining and Consecrating of Bishops, Priests and Deacons; and in the Thirty-nine Articles of Religion and to transmit the same unimpaired to our posterity.

In 1918 the Church of England in Canada issued its own *Book of Common Prayer* which was remarkably identical to the 1662 Prayer Book. However, "the General Synod of the Church of England in Canada determined to make such adaptations and enrichments in the body of the Book" as would reflect "many changes [that] have taken place in the life of the Church and its outlook upon the world." On the Eucharist, though, the Canadian Church maintained the 1662 Eucharistic Prayer along with the

Black Rubric that declared *"no Adoration is intended, or ought to be done, either unto the Sacramental Bread or Wine there bodily received, or unto any Corporal Presence of Christ's natural Flesh and Blood. For the Sacramental Bread and Wine remain in their natural substances, and therefore may not be adored; (for that were Idolatry, to be abhorred of all faithful Christians)."*

The 1962 *Book of Common Prayer* made some significant changes in the Communion rite, patterning it on the Church of England's 1928 Proposed Prayer Book, but excluding any epiclesis, or calling on the Holy Spirit "to bless and sanctify the gifts of bread and wine to be unto us the Body and Blood of Christ." Evangelicals in the church strongly opposed any such inclusion and it was dropped from the Communion rite. On the other hand, a move to replace the word "memory" with "memorial" was accepted, and so the rite reads: "….and did institute and in his holy Gospel command us to continue, a perpetual memorial of that his precious death, until his coming again."

The debate about "memory" or "memorial" is an interesting one. Memory is a more dynamic word, encompassing both past and present, and more accurate in reflecting the Greek word "anamnesis" which is often translated as "remembrance." Memorial is more objective, fixed, permanent and even static. One thinks of a "memorial" for a past event or person, for example, the Vietnam Memorial or the Lincoln Memorial in Washington, D.C. Even today, we think of a "memorial service" for someone who is dead. And yet, the resurrected Jesus is a living Lord transcending time and space. Memory transcends boundaries of past and present, and is, therefore, a more appropriate word to use in the Eucharist.

There were other changes in the 1962 Communion Service. The Prayer of Humble Access was moved from before the consecration to after the peace, but the Lord's Prayer remained after reception of communion. The Black Rubric was retained in a modified form that eliminated the characterization of "Idolatry" for any adoration of the consecrated Bread and Wine. Still, the Black Rubric declared *the Body of Christ is given, taken and eaten, in the Supper, only after an heavenly and spiritual manner. And the mean whereby the Body of Christ is received and eaten in the Supper is Faith."* This was in keeping with the belief, prevalent in Canada, that the presence of Christ in the sacrament is spiritual and not corporal: in eating the bread and drinking the wine, we receive Christ by faith.

This doctrine of "spiritual communion by faith" was reiterated in the section on The Ministry to the Sick. The rubric at the end of Section IV (page 584) gave this pastoral assurance to a person unable to receive communion by mouth:

> *But if a man, by reason of extreme sickness… do not receive the Sacrament of Christ's Body and Blood: he shall be instructed that if he do truly repent him of his sins, and steadfastly believe that Jesus Christ hath suffered death upon the Cross for him, and shed his Blood for his redemption, earnestly remembering the benefits he hath thereby, and giving him hearty thanks therefor; he doth eat and drink the Body and Blood of our Saviour Christ profitably to his soul's health, although he do not receive the Sacrament with his mouth.*

In addition to the Communion Service, the Confession in both Morning and Evening Prayer was modified, striking the phrases in the 1662 Prayer Book: "…provoking most justly thy wrath and indignation against us. …the remembrance of them is grievous unto us; the burden of them is intolerable." Similarly, in the Confession at Communion, the term "miserable offenders" was stricken. Apparently, even sin for Anglicans had its limits.

Finally, the 1962 Prayer Book added additional services not found in the 1662 book such as: The Form of Institution and Induction of a Rector; The Laying of a Foundation Stone of a Church or Chapel; the Consecration of a Church or Chapel; An Order of Compline; Family Prayers and a Form of Prayer to be Used at Sea. The Eucharistic lectionary was basically the same as the 1662 Prayer Book, but the Daily Office lectionary was an adaptation of the English 1928 Proposed Book of Common Prayer that was never approved. In addition, as an alternative to reciting all 150 psalms in thirty days, the Prayer Book provided for an optional sixty day recitation.

All in all, the 1962 Canadian Prayer Book reflected continuity and change with past Prayer Books. A casual observer would not notice any major alterations, except for a longer Prayer of Consecration. The look, feel and composition was thoroughly traditional. In adopting the book, Canadian Anglicans felt they had given a gift to the worldwide Anglican

Communion. However, just as the book was being adopted, the first session of Vatican II was about to commence.

# Questions

1. Do you think that the debate between Samuel Seabury and William White continues in the Episcopal Church today between "traditionalist" and "progressive" factions in the church? In what way?

2. How much agreement should there be in a congregation or a diocese for people to be in communion with one another?

3. Does it bother you that some of your fellow worshipers may not believe in the Eucharist the same way that you do? Do you think everyone should believe the same things in order to worship the same way? Explain your answer.

# SESSION 9

# THE OXFORD MOVEMENT AND LITURGICAL RENEWAL

*And now again we exhort you, in the Name of our Lord Jesus Christ, that you have in remembrance into how high a dignity, and to how weighty an office and charge ye are called: That is to say, to be messengers, watchmen, and stewards of the Lord; to teach and to premonish, to feed and provide for the Lord's family; to seek for Christ's sheep that are dispersed abroad, and for his children who are in the midst of this naughty world, that they may be saved through Christ forever. – Address of the bishop to the ordinands for the priesthood in the Ordinal of the 1662 Book of Common Prayer*

*If Christ is the Priest for our souls, let us beware of ever giving His office to another. Let no man delude us into supposing that we need any clergyman, or minister, or priest, of any Church on earth, to be our spiritual director and soul's confessor. ...Occasional private conferences with a minister is one thing; habitual confession of sin, with habitual absolution, is quite another. ...Ministers are useful just so far as they promote private communion between Jesus Christ and our souls. But the moment a minister begins to stand between our soul and Christ, even in the slightest degree, he becomes an enemy and not a friend to our peace.... No priest but Christ! – Bishop J.C. Ryle, Knots Untied (1874)*

From 1662 to the mid-nineteenth century, the Church of England was settled in its form of worship. The 1662 *Book of Common Prayer* was embedded in the mindset and practice of the English people. It was the only authorized worship book, and failure to use it or to misuse it was a civil as well as canonical offense. Worship itself varied very little from church to church, with Communion celebrated three to six times a year in most parishes, though Collegiate churches celebrated Communion every Sunday and Feast Day. The worship was plain, simple and without any undue ceremonial. There was no cross or candles on the Communion Table. Priests celebrated from the "North End" in cassock, surplice and tippet without any kneeling, bowing or hand gestures other than what was prescribed in the Prayer Book. All this began to change in the nineteenth century with the rise of the Oxford Movement.

## I. The Oxford Movement and the Rise of Ritualism

The Oxford Movement officially commenced on July 14, 1833, with a sermon preached by John Keble in the University Church of St. Mary the Virgin. It was a call for the Church of England to reclaim its Catholic roots in the face of the challenges of modernity – secularism, pluralism, atheism and scientism.

Although the Oxford Movement originally focused on theology, polity and devotional life, it gradually expanded to include worship, ritual, ceremonial, church architecture and music. Many adherents of the Oxford Movement viewed the Middle Ages as the high point of Christianity, and they took all things Roman as their model. Church architecture was employed to highlight Catholic theology by elaborate altars and ornate rood screens which had been removed from churches at the time of the Reformation. Instead of the simple cassock, surplice and tippet, priests began wearing chasubles, stoles and other colored vestments that had not been worn by Anglican clergy since the first part of the sixteenth century.

> Vestments are not an issue in the Episcopal Church in the United States, the Anglican Church of Canada, and in most churches of the Anglican Communion. Officially, clerical dress has no theological significance, though clergy often wear vestments that express their priestly views. Those who wear cassock, surplice and tippet in celebrating Holy Communion usually have quite a different view of the priesthood from those who wear Roman or medieval vestments. When clergy gather together for a diocesan event, it is quite interesting to observe what they are wearing. Their vestments usually symbolize what they believe about the priesthood.

The Oxford Movement began as a Catholic reform of the Church of England. However, some of its more partisan adherents, such as John Henry

Newman in his Tract 90, attempted to interpret the English Reformation in a way not inconsistent with Roman Catholic theology. The standard for the church was not the Articles of Religion, but the Council of Trent. Inevitably, a movement that so valued Rome and the Middle Ages began to focus on externals in worship, liturgy and church life. Opponents of the Oxford Movement labeled the focus on externals 'ritualism' – an obsession with elaborate ceremonial.

Proponents of ritualism had a romantic view of the medieval church and rejected Reformation doctrine. Ritualists looked to the Roman Catholic Church as an authoritative source of doctrinal and liturgical truth, with clergy claiming to celebrate 'High Mass' with their back to the people, robed in elaborate vestments, using incense, with candles and a cross on the altar. Ritualism led to gradual adoption of a comprehensively sacramental system, including a movement away from 'a real but spiritual presence' to a belief that Christ's presence in the Eucharist was objectively real in the bread and wine. Some Anglo-Catholic parishes began celebrating Benediction which entailed the adoration of the consecrated Host in a monstrance – an open transparent receptacle in which the consecrated Host is exposed for veneration.

Roman Catholics often were perplexed by Anglo-Catholic ritualists. It seemed as if these Anglo-Catholics were trying to be more Roman than the Romans in their liturgical practices. In response, Anglo-Catholics claimed they were Catholics, but not Roman Catholics. That, of course, was what they claimed, but were they really Catholics in a substantive way or just Catholics in form only? Roman Catholics maintained that to be a true Catholic, one had to be in communion with the Pope – the See of Peter – and on that the Anglo-Catholics demurred, except John Henry Newman, Frederick William Faber, Henry Manning and those who eventually converted to the Roman Catholic Church.

> The nineteenth century Anglo-Catholics were in many
> ways no different from Bishops Stephen Gardiner,
> Cuthbert Tunstall and Edmond Bonner during the reign
> of King Henry VIII. They justified the schism with Rome
> by claiming they remained Catholic, but not Roman
> Catholic. Their arguments seemed legitimate until the
> reign of Edward VI when it was clear that the Church
> of England would embark on a thorough reform. The
> three bishops renounced their schismatic positions and
> were restored to favor under the reign of the Catholic
> Queen Mary. They came to understand that what
> ensures a Catholic Church is more than rite and ceremony
> but a firm doctrinal authority that is embodied in the
> Bishop of Rome, the Pope, who as the successor of
> St. Peter, holds the keys to the kingdom of heaven.

Were the Anglo-Catholics attempting to revise church history or pretend that the Reformation never happened? In form, yes, but not necessarily in substance. There were few Anglo-Catholics, outside of those who converted to the Roman Catholic Church, who accepted transubstantiation. While Anglo-Catholics insisted on a real presence of Christ in the Eucharist, they were content to leave the details of how Christ is made present as a mystery. Nineteenth century Tractarians, in particular, upheld the importance of the sacrament while generally rejecting transubstantiation. Some, like Edward Pusey, an original member of the Oxford Movement and leading Tractarian, preferred consubstantiation in which "the true flesh and blood of Christ are in the true bread and wine – the two are so mingled that they constitute one thing."[1] In this view, the bread and wine do not disappear at the consecration, but the Body and Blood become present without diminishing them.

The Bishop Gloucester Edgar Gibson had Anglo-Catholic sympathies. And yet, in his book on the Thirty-nine Articles of Religion, he defended the statement in Article XXVIII that "Transubstantiation… cannot be proved by Holy Writ; but is repugnant to the plain words of Scripture, overthroweth the nature of a Sacrament, and hath given occasion to many superstitions." Bishop Gibson wrote:

> It is hard to see how a philosophical theory such as Transubstantiation confessedly is, can ever be "proved by Holy Writ." Romanists point to the words of institution… But though they can certainly be claimed in the favour of the real Presence, yet to bring into them a theory of "accidents" remaining while the "substance" is changed, is to read into the text that which is certainly not contained in it, and what we deny can reasonably be referred from it.[2]

Anglo-Catholics continued to influence the Church of England, and especially the American Episcopal Church, in ritual, ceremony and architecture. Most Episcopal churches, for example, from the latter part of the 19th century were constructed in a Gothic or Romanesque style of architecture, looking more like a medieval building than a modern one. The Christopher Wren or federal style of church architecture was largely abandoned. Instead of bright, spacious open churches with the Lord's Prayer, the Ten Commandments and the Apostles' Creed prominently displayed, churches were now dark, somber spaces with the high altar (made of stone or marble, not wood) far from the people and separated from the congregation by choir stalls and a rood screen. Oddly enough, most Episcopalians did not like Anglo-Catholic theology, but they were attracted to the Gothic or Romanesque architecture, the bright colored stained-glass windows, the elaborate altars, and the feeling of being in a medieval church in a nineteenth or twentieth century world. It wasn't theology but aesthetics that pulled Episcopalians towards ritualism.

Still, Anglo-Catholic theology managed to influence the church. The Parish Communion Movement promoted the Eucharist as the central act of worship in the church, and as a result almost every Anglican and Episcopal church in the twentieth century started an early morning Eucharist as a complement to Morning Prayer at the main service. Fasting before communion became a common spiritual discipline for some churchgoers. Anglo-Catholic churches began offering private confession to a priest and to reserve the 'Blessed Sacrament' in tabernacles for worshippers to adore when there was no Eucharist. The intellectual emphasis of the Reformation gave way to a mystical ethos in the liturgy where God was more to be experienced and encountered than known and understood.

> Protestantism, especially Calvinism, is a religion of the mind, which is why the sermon holds the central place in worship, with the pulpit often at the center of the chancel, replacing the old altar. The communion table, if at all present, is positioned below the pulpit. The symbolism is unmistakable: the Word has precedence over the Sacrament. In contrast, Roman Catholicism is a religion of the heart. Roman Catholic churches have the altar as the main focus of attention, with the pulpit on the side, and not nearly as imposing a structure. Here the sermon is preparation for what is the central and primary act of worship – the Holy Sacrifice of the Mass in which the sacrifice of Christ is renewed by the actions of the priest who acts "in personae Christi" – in the person of Christ.

## II. The 1928 Proposed Book of Common Prayer

The influence of the Oxford Movement and Anglo-Catholicism led to an attempt to revise the 1662 Prayer Book. In 1928, a new *Book of Common Prayer* was proposed by leaders of the Church of England. While the book itself was not a radical change from the 1662 book, there were just enough changes to set off a firestorm of opposition from both evangelicals and traditionalists. The book would move the Church of England in a decidedly Catholic direction.

On the surface, the Proposed 1928 book read and felt remarkably similar to the 1662 book. The language was still Cranmer's. Most of the rites of 1662 were maintained, including Morning and Evening Prayer and the Communion Service. However, there was intense opposition over several new rites included in the proposed book.

1. The rite for The Communion of the Sick included rubrics that provided for the "*consecrated Bread and Wine thus set apart shall be reserved in an aumbry or safe.*" The purpose for this reservation was so that "*the consecrated Bread and Wine are taken from the church to the sick person before the priest administers the Holy Sacrament…*" Another rubric made clear that reservation is "only for the Communion of the Sick" and "*shall be used for no other purpose whatsoever.*" Despite a clear prohibition about using the

reserved sacrament for any other purpose, the fear of evangelicals was the bread and wine would be used for purposes of adoration or worship, such as Benediction practiced in the Roman Catholic Church. Even the idea of reserving the sacrament was abhorrent to some Anglicans who still thought that any real presence of Christ by means of the bread and wine ended with the Communion Service, and therefore there was nothing to reserve.

2. While the 1662 Order of Communion was retained, including the Black Rubric at the end of the service, an Alternative Order for the Administration of the Lord's Supper was included that prolonged the consecration prayer after the words of institution. It also had the Lord's Prayer before the reception of communion rather than afterwards. This made the gap between consecration and reception even longer, and frustrated Cranmer's intention that reception and not the consecration should be the climax of the service. Moreover, the proposed Prayer of Consecration included an *epiclesis*: "Hear us, O merciful Father, we most humbly beseech thee, and with thy Holy and Life-giving Spirit vouchsafe to bless and sanctify both us and these thy gifts of Bread and Wine, that they may be unto us the Body and Blood of thy Son, our Saviour, Jesus Christ..." Evangelicals strongly opposed any *epiclesis* because it implied a kind of spiritual transformation of the elements that came too close to resembling transubstantiation. For evangelicals, it wasn't the elements that mattered so much as the reception of the elements by faith.

3. The Burial of the Dead included explicit prayers for the dead. This was done as a pastoral response to the intense grief of people who lost loved ones in the First World War. The massive number of casualties was staggering and people felt a need to commend their loved ones to God, to pray for them, and to ask God's mercy upon them. However, evangelicals were adamantly against any such provision, the reason being that prayers for the dead implied an intermediate state between earth and heaven – a kind of purgatory that was explicitly condemned by Article XXII of the Articles of Religion. When you are dead, you go to heaven or hell – the decision is made, the judgment is final. So why pray for

the dead? Prayers for the dead implied an intermediate state that was inconsistent with traditional Anglican belief.

There were many commendable things in the 1928 Prayer Book, including alternate versions of Morning and Evening Prayer, Services of Prime and Compline, and an alternative lectionary. The book referred to the First Day of Lent as Ash Wednesday and the Sunday Next Before Easter as Palm Sunday. It included additional prayers for various occasions but maintained the Eucharistic collects and readings for Sundays and Feast Days. It was a balanced and well-organized book that undoubtedly would have enriched the worship of the Church of England.

The Church of England is an established church. The Monarch is the Supreme Governor of the Church, and Parliament had, by law, to approve the book. The debate in Parliament was intense. Members who were never considered 'religious' or having any strong opinions about the church, voiced opposition to the book. In the end, the measure to approve the proposed *Book of Common Prayer* went down to defeat, and so to this day the 1662 Prayer Book remains the official worship book of the Church of England.

That, however, would not end the desire for liturgical reform. Soon after the defeat, bishops began allowing certain parts of the book to be used for worship as a supplement to the official Prayer Book. Although defeated by Parliament, the 1928 Prayer Book would have significant influence throughout the Anglican world, and the 1962 Canadian *Book of Common Prayer* relied heavily on it.

The 1662 *Book of Common Prayer* has to this day its devoted supporters, and even evangelicals from other denominations value the book and use it in their personal devotions. In 2021, InterVarsity Press published an International Edition of the 1662 *Book of Common Prayer* that revised outdated spellings and phraseologies, removed references to the British Monarchy and Royal Family, replacing them with more generic state prayers, and gave the book a more modern look and feel, while retaining the services and language. Additional prayers were added for personal devotions, the Articles of Religion were retained, and the sixteenth century Homily of Justification was included. The new book was the work of Gerald Bray, a British Anglican scholar who is now a professor at Beeson

University in the United States. Clearly the 1662 *Book of Common Prayer* refuses to die, and it remains a pillar of traditional Anglican worship and belief.

## III. The Liturgical Movement

The Proposed 1928 *Book of Common Prayer* did not originate out of the blue. The Roman Catholic Church was undergoing its own move for liturgical reform, though in a more restrained way. Although it never had an official name, it is often known as the 'Liturgical Movement' and it was initiated by French Benedictine monks in the nineteenth century who wanted to renew worship along the lines of the early church. In Anglicanism, the Liturgical Movement desired to restore active participation of the people in worship, to make baptism full initiation into the church, and to have the Holy Eucharist as the principal act of the church's worship.

The English liturgist A.G. Hebert (1886 – 1963) popularized the movement with his books *Liturgy and Society* (1935) and *The Parish Communion Movement* (1937). Hebert challenged the classic shape of Sunday morning Anglican worship which, until the 1890s, tended to be Morning Prayer, Litany, and Ante-communion (the Communion service up to the Prayers of the People), with Communion four to six times a year. Hebert and his proponents challenged that structure so that by the 1950s a typical Anglican or Episcopal church would have an early morning Communion service, with the main service being Morning Prayer three Sundays a month and Communion once a month. However, the goal was to have the Eucharist celebrated at the main Sunday service at every church throughout the world.

Hebert emphasized the social character of the Eucharist in contrast to the individualism of Morning Prayer. He wrote eloquently of the theology of liturgical mystery, of the whole people of God, and of self-offering in response to God's self-offering in Jesus. Although not well known by the typical Anglican, his works proved highly influential in connecting liturgy with life, belief with behavior, and receiving the Body of Christ with being the Body of Christ in the world.

Dom Gregory Dix (1901 – 1952) was more influential than Hebert because of his monumental book *The Shape of the Liturgy* (1945). Dix was a British Benedictine monk who argued that the Eucharist is an action that has a fourfold shape corresponding to the actions of Jesus at the Last Supper: taking, blessing, breaking and giving the bread and cup – offertory, prayer, fraction and communion. This was an important contribution to liturgical renewal, though some scholars have criticized the book as lacking historical accuracy.

However, Dix did more than argue for the four-fold shape of the Eucharist. His book was a vitriolic attack on Thomas Cranmer and his liturgy. He claimed, "Cranmer in his eucharistic doctrine was a devout and theologically founded Zwinglian, and that his Prayer Books were exactly framed to express his convictions."[3] While this view of Cranmer is controversial, it is correct, as most evangelical Anglicans would admit, such as Bishop Colin Buchanan and Diarmuid McCulloch.

Dom Gregory Dix, A.G. Hebert and the Parish Communion Movement all influenced Anglican theology and liturgy. However, the greatest influence on Anglican liturgical renewal came from outside the Anglican world. This happened when an old and rather frail Pope John XXIII, who many expected to be a mere caretaker Pope, decided to call a church council.

Vatican II changed the face of liturgical reform with its sweeping move to put the Latin Mass into the vernacular, abolish the Tridentine rite and replace it with a new Eucharistic rite with several consecration prayers.

The move was more radical than just a change of language. The Tridentine Mass was replaced by entirely new forms of worship that sent shockwaves through the Roman Catholic world. As one Catholic priest said in exasperation, "Almost overnight, we have gone from Gregorian Chant to Kumbaya." The noted historian Garry Wills has characterized the period after Vatican II as a time of "bare ruined choirs" because so many priests began leaving the church and attendance at the new vernacular Mass dropped dramatically. If Roman Catholics thought that liturgical renewal would bring more people to church, they were wrong. It had the opposite effect.

However, when the Roman Catholic Church acts, the rest of Christendom feels compelled to respond. Anglicans now felt a need to renew their own liturgies in a way that would appeal to the modern world much as Roman Catholics were doing. It is doubtful how many Anglicans wanted to embark on liturgical renewal, but the actions of the Roman Catholic Church forced their hand.

## IV. New Prayer Books

No Anglican Church around the world was affected more by the liturgical changes set forth by Vatican II than the Anglican Church of Canada. The church had just authorized a new Prayer Book in 1962, and yet almost immediately it was perceived as outdated. American Episcopalians, on the other hand, used a Prayer Book dating back to 1928, and most members recognized it was time to update their book, though few could have envisioned the end result.

The 1979 *Book of Common Prayer* included worship and prayers in both Rite I traditional language and Rite II contemporary language. It reflected the liturgical developments of Vatican II and the Liturgical Movement, making the Eucharist the principal act of worship and Baptism as full membership in the church. It was the longest Prayer Book ever compiled, containing a large selection of prayers and forms of worship, with many options for the Daily Offices and Eucharist.

After the Prayer Book was approved by General Convention, new Prayer Books and other worship resources began to appear in Anglican Churches around the world. These books reflected the thinking of the Liturgical Movement, but also the Oxford Movement. In structure and format, they were much closer to the Roman Catholic structure than at any time since the Reformation. However, in theology, the books maintained a balance between Catholic and Reformed elements, and all were ambiguous on key points of doctrine so that most of the liturgies would be acceptable to both Anglo-Catholics and Evangelicals.

- *The 1980 Authorized Service Book (ASB) of the Church of England* was more conservative in theology and less radical in its forms of contemporary worship, reflecting a mildly reformed and evangelical perspective thanks to the influence of Bishop Colin Buchanan.

- ***The 1985 Book of Alternative Services (BAS) of the Anglican Church of Canada*** went further than the ASB of the Church of England with thoroughly contemporary liturgy, while including a modest amount of traditional worship. The BAS took much of its liturgy from the American Episcopal Church, including the psalms and lectionary, while retaining a distinctly Canadian ethos. A chief criticism of this book has been that it substitutes the liturgical language of Cranmer for a modern idiom which neither uplifts nor inspires the spirit.

- ***The 1989 New Zealand Prayer Book*** was by far the most far-reaching, not only using contemporary language but radically revising the traditional prayers and forms of worship including a verbose and convoluted interpretation of the Lord's Prayer. It is a well-designed book and cutting-edge for its time with a fairly radical theological orientation in a contemporary idiom. The problem is that a 'trendy' book may be fresh and relevant in one generation but become quickly outdated in another. As G.K. Chesterton wisely observed: "He who marries the spirit of the times will soon find himself a widower."

- ***The 2000 Common Worship of the Church of England*** and its subsequent publications assumes that we now live in a digital world where forms of worship can be altered or mixed according to the context. The book includes many options but no theological consistency. Critics have charged that the book is too ambiguous on key points of Anglican theology, especially on the Eucharist.

Despite the varied Prayer Books in the churches of the Anglican Communion, liturgists appear to agree that there are common elements to Anglican worship – not so much in theology (where there is wide disagreement) but in form and structure. Continuity with the historic Anglican tradition would have these characteristics:

1. A clear structure for worship.
2. The public reading of the Scriptures in the language of the people, and instruction based on them.

3. Liturgical words repeated by the congregation, some of which, like the Lord's Prayer, would be known by heart.
4. The use of two sacraments, Baptism and Holy Communion.
5. Episcopal ordination of all three Orders of Ministry – deacon, priest and bishop – with the laying on of hands.
6. A concern for form, dignity, and an economy of words.

Yet even these characteristics seem inadequate, given that the world around us is changing rapidly and the forces of secularism are fast impinging on church and culture. Anglicans need to have more than a common structure if we are to transform lives in Jesus Christ. Form over substance will not do.

> Today we may legitimately ask, "How does the church reach a culture where most people are no longer familiar with the Christian story or do not know it accurately?" To answer that question, we must move beyond worship to mission in what is being called the MISSIONAL CHURCH or an EMERGING CHURCH or even a NEW APOSTOLIC CHURCH.

Anglicans like to think of the Prayer Book as a book for all people. However, it has never been a book for all people, not even in sixteenth century England when both Catholics and Puritans opposed it. Yet, the myth remains that Anglicanism has the capacity to minister to a diversity of people. We think of ourselves as a church of common prayer, in which different people of different backgrounds come together and become one in receiving Christ's Body and Blood in Holy Communion. But what about the increasing number of people who are not baptized, or know little or nothing about Christianity? Both in the United States and Canada, there is increasing demographic fragmentation. How can any church possibly hope to minister to everyone using the same book? We need to abandon a "one size fits all" model of ministry and shape our worship to reach different types of people at their own level of need and understanding. In the future, worship will be targeted to specific demographic groups rather than be generic. This may well mean revising the Prayer Book more often than Anglicans are accustomed to do, or at least offering supplemental liturgies on a regular basis.

The twenty-first century presents the American Episcopal and Canadian Anglican Churches with the greatest missionary challenge since the conversion of Europe. Bridging the gap between Christendom and post-Christendom will be difficult but not impossible. The Prayer Book will always have a place in our worship but Anglicans and Episcopalians need not be enslaved to it. Local churches, in particular, will need to expand their worship to reach an emerging world that is mission territory. We need a kind of 'worship evangelism' that would have been unimaginable in Cranmer's day. The church must seek the positive meaning of what is happening in the culture by grappling with the question: **HOW DOES THE CHURCH BEST RESPOND TO WHAT GOD IS DOING IN THE WORLD TODAY?** That is the key question we must answer, and with it how the Prayer Book fits into that response.

## Questions

1.  How important is correct doctrine or "orthodoxy" for the life of the church?
2.  How do you react to liturgical renewal? Are you a person who values liturgical variation and change, or do you prefer a more fixed and set way of worshipping? Do you think a Prayer Book could accommodate both ways?
3.  How should the church handle things that are not explicitly mentioned in the Bible (like race relations, immigration, global warming and nuclear warfare)?

# SESSION 10

# THE FUTURE OF PRAYER BOOK WORSHIP

*Worship points steadily towards the reality of God: gives, expresses, and maintains that which is the essence of all sane religion – a theocentric basis of life. The first or central act of religion is adoration, the sense of God, his otherness through nearness, his distinctness from all finite beings though not separateness – aloofness – from them. In this great sanctus, all things justify their being and have their place. God alone matters, God alone is – creation only matters because of God. – Evelyn Underhill, Worship (1936)*

*Remember that Christianity is not, first and foremost, a religion; it is first and foremost a revelation. It comes before us chiefly not with a declaration of feelings we are to cultivate, or thoughts we are to develop; it comes before us, first and foremost, with the announcement of what God is, as He is proved in what he has done. – Archbishop William Temple, Nature, Man and God (1935)*

*The Book of Common Prayer* in its successive editions in England and around the world has shaped a distinctly Anglican way of being Christian. The Prayer Book is more than a Missal or a worship resource. It is, in fact, the closest thing to a definitive authority, encompassing what Anglicans believe as well as how they worship.

Throughout the pages of the Prayer Book we find a balanced, sane, and thoughtful kind of religion that is deeply respectful of tradition and values the language of holiness, yet speaks to every generation with timeless truths taken directly from Holy Scripture. We enter into the mystery and majesty of God, not to understand it as much as to be transformed by it. In the encounter with God we are challenged as well as comforted, disturbed as well as assured, and forced to examine our lives in light of our faith. There is in the Prayer Book the recognition that truth is not simple, but sacred; and that spiritual maturity involves many virtues including humility, patience, the ability to leave doubtful things doubtful, and toleration. This willingness to enter into the mystery of God is at the heart of Anglican worship.

## I. Ten Characteristics of Prayer Book Worship

There is no one Prayer Book but many Prayer Books, from different centuries and from different churches of the Anglican Communion. The Prayer Book of the Anglican Church of Canada, for example, is not the same as the Prayer Book of the Episcopal Church in the United States. Each church within the Anglican Communion has its own distinctive identity, and yet, there is a commonality to every book.

1. **Common Prayer.** *The Book of Common Prayer* is a worship book for the whole church. It is a book that shapes, defines and gives the church its self-understanding as a worshipping community. It provides common patterns of worship that affirm common life. These common worship patterns enable Christians from different congregations to recognize each other as part of one church. Moreover, common worship patterns also enable Christians who may not agree with each other theologically to share in the same worship, to eat from the same table, and to pray as one community. Anglicans need not believe the same things in the same way to worship at the same table. Despite our differences, there is, what Richard Hooker called, God's "harmonious dissimilitude." Common prayer guards against a closed and excluding spirit. It increases tolerance for those who may think differently or even behave differently from ourselves. It allows us to live and accept our differences united by common rituals that draw us closer to God.

2. **Ownership by the People.** Worship, as Anglicans understand it, is something done by priest and people together. Unlike Roman Catholicism, there are no private Masses in Anglicanism celebrated by the priest alone. The principle of participation by the whole people of God is essential for common prayer. Participation demands that corporate worship be celebrated in the common tongue, because worship must always be intelligible to those who

share in it. Moreover, because the laity along with the clergy have access to the Prayer Book, both orders are accountable to each other in the performance of the liturgy.

3. **Consensus in Development.** *The Book of Common Prayer* is not imposed on the church by an ecclesiastical hierarchy, but one that reflects wide support by members of the church. In fact, there can be no Prayer Book in any Anglican Church without the approval of both laity and clergy. A curious result of the Reformation doctrine of the "priesthood of all believers" was that Archbishop Cranmer's Prayer Books were authorized by Parliament, which saw itself as the lay voice of the church – a kind of lay synod that counterbalanced the power of clergy. This process implies that the laity can be sufficiently informed and sufficiently trusted to make decisions in doctrinal matters affecting the church. It was Erasmus of Rotterdam who wisely observed that all can be Christians, all can be devout, and all can be theologians.

4. **Balanced Theology.** Anglicanism from at least the seventeenth century attempted to steer a middle course (via media) between two extremes, avoiding the excesses of the Roman Catholics on the one hand, and the Puritans on the other. It aimed to restore all that was sound and right, and to celebrate it in the balanced and beautiful prose of the liturgy. Even today, the Prayer Book is designed to be biblical teaching in liturgical form embracing the whole of life. It is a worship book both Catholic and Reformed; Catholic in that it reflects the essentials of Catholic faith dating back to the time of the apostles; Reformed because medieval accretions are eliminated, the criterion being that nothing is to be allowed contrary to Scripture. This balance in Anglicanism is sometimes hard to maintain, but it is essential to the church's identity. Ideally, Anglicanism is not Catholic only or Protestant only, but Catholic and Protestant at one and the same time. In order to be more truly Catholic, the church is always called to be more Protestant and Reformed – what is often termed a reformed Catholicism.

5. **Intentional Ambiguity.** *The Book of Common Prayer* is deliberately formulated to allow a wide variety of theologies under the Anglican

umbrella. Anglicans of vastly different theological persuasions are able to worship with the same book, participate in the same acts, and receive the same bread and wine at Holy Communion, even if they have different understandings of what they are doing. Queen Elizabeth I, for example, decreed that neither civil nor ecclesiastical authorities must pry into the conscience of her subjects. So long as they attended worship and received Holy Communion, that was enough to demonstrate their loyalty to Church and Crown, whatever their personal convictions. So today, anyone who wants to worship in an Anglican church is always welcome.

6. **The Language of Prayer.** *The Book of Common Prayer* has shaped the language of personal devotion through public and personal use. Along with the words of Shakespeare and the King James Version of the Bible, the Prayer Book is one of the jewels of the English language. The power and poetry of words and phrases is taken very seriously as a way of involving both heart and mind in prayer. The Prayer Book has entered deep into the memories of generations of people, and so has become a dearly loved book around which the church is formed. Much of the power of Anglican liturgical forms arises from the attempt to harness the moods and processes of all the joys and pains of being human. Some of these cycles reflect the struggle between sin and grace as life moves between lament and liberation, penitence and celebration, memory and hope, forgiveness and new life. The Prayer Book takes the most significant aspects of living and shapes them into prayer.

7. **Lex Orandi, Lex Credendi.** The relationship between worship and belief is often discussed under the Latin tag, *lex ordandi, lex credendi* – prayer and belief are integral to one another, and therefore liturgy is not distinct from theology. It was Archbishop Michael Ramsey who recognized how Anglican belief and thought has developed under the sound of church bells, with worship, prayer, doctrine and practice interrelated and informing each other. It was Ramsey who said that if you want to understand us, come worship with us. Thus, doctrine and worship come together in *The Book of Common Prayer*. To know what Anglicans believe is to see how Anglicans worship. Without spelling out precisely how

we are to believe particular Christian truths, Anglican worship nonetheless directs our thinking about God, salvation, life, the world, the church, behavior, and everything else. We set it all within the framework of worship.

8. **A Wide Variety of Ceremonial.** Both 'high' and 'low' church coexist together using the same book. Go into one Anglican church at worship, and it may resemble a Roman Mass before Vatican II. Go into another Anglican church at worship, and the service may be plain and simple, more akin to a Methodist or Presbyterian church. Yet, each church uses the same book. How can this be? Comprehensiveness or inclusivity are very much a part of Anglicanism. We are a church of both/and rather than either/or. We make room for a wide variety of ceremonial, using the same book, saying the same words, reading from the same Scripture lessons, and praying to the same God. A fundamental principle of Anglican worship is unity in essentials, liberty in non-essentials, and charity in all things.

9. **Stability.** People find in the Prayer Book familiar liturgical shapes and verbal landmarks in worship. Prayer Book worship tends to be predictable, fixed and structured, which results in a high degree of comfort for people harried by the changes in the world. Admittedly, this stability also can seem boring: too routine, too monotonous and repetitious, especially to younger generations. There are challenges here, to be sure, especially how the church ministers effectively to people who have grown-up in a digital, fast-paced, constantly changing world. However, it was Archbishop Cranmer's intention in developing the First (1549) and Second (1552) Prayer Books to produce a liturgy that would unite both church and nation in worship. In order to have common prayer for the entire nation, it was essential to have prayer that was indeed common – thus the need for stability.

10. **Sacramental Religion.** The Prayer Book affirms that God can use the natural, physical and human as the vehicle for what is supernatural, spiritual and divine. Spoken words, physical touch, even humble inanimate matter like water, bread and wine can be channels of God's love, power and grace. Sacramental religion

promotes a sacramental view of life: the interdependence of creation in a common dependence on the Creator. It draws us out of ourselves into the world around us. It proclaims that all created things are outward and visible signs of inward and spiritual grace. That there is nothing created which is not good; and there is nothing good which is not called to be holy.

## II. A Prayer Book Church in a Twenty-first Century World

Although Prayer Book worship has survived for almost 500 hundred years, it is now under enormous challenges. A post-modern culture is impatient with fixed forms, repetitious liturgical rites, and print worship. A post-Christian culture no longer understands, much less appreciates, the rich biblical symbolism contained in the Prayer Book. A secular culture may dismiss religion entirely, feeling no need or having no interest in being part of any church.

In re-evaluating the Prayer Book for twenty-first century North America, Anglicans will need to answer three questions.

1. **Can Prayer Book worship effectively connect with a post-Christian culture?** *The Book of Common Prayer* was developed in Christendom where the language of faith was widely known and universally accepted. Prayer Book worship may not work as well in an increasingly unchurched and biblically illiterate culture where people do not know the language of faith. If, one of the stated reasons for *The Book of Common Prayer* was that worship should be in the language of the people, then how does the language of the Prayer Book connect with North American culture today? Is the language, and even the forms of worship, becoming obsolete? Or might this intentionally antiquarian worship be the vehicle that draws seekers into an encounter with the mystery that is God?

2. **Has technology made Prayer Book worship obsolete?** The Prayer Book would not have been possible without the technology of the time: the invention of the printing press. In the digital age,

is a new kind of worship emerging that will make Anglicanism's reliance on the printed page obsolete? The proliferation of tablets, e-readers and smart phones suggest that people are developing a new way of processing information – away from the printed page and onto an electronic screen. It is not uncommon today to hear people say that they have gone "paperless" – all their records and receipts are now stored on computers and electronic devices. Does all this mean that in the future Anglicanism will no longer be a Prayer Book church?

3. **Is a *Book of Common Prayer* possible given the increasing theological, cultural and political pluralism in the church?** Common Prayer depends on a common faith, but the church's growing theological pluralism is increasingly making common prayer difficult. It is problematic whether there will continue to be patterns of prayer which unite Anglicans of different backgrounds, political persuasions and theological viewpoints. "Inclusiveness" is a word many Anglicans cherish, but how far does inclusiveness extend? How wide is wide before the church moves beyond the historic Christian faith? Are there limits, parameters and boundaries that the church must retain? If so, what is at the heart of our faith that is non-negotiable? How can we formulate common liturgical language without a common core of belief?

Anglicanism was birthed in Christendom when the social, political, economic and legal life of the nation was intertwined with the church. Queen Elizabeth I was declared Supreme Governor of the Church. Citizenship and church membership were integrally connected, so that it was inconceivable that one could be a loyal citizen of England without being a member of the Church of England.

How different is the world today where the separation of church and state is taken for granted. Even England with an established church, is a multi-religious, multi-cultural, pluralistic nation. Today the culture is moving in a direction unimaginable just twenty or thirty years ago that make it increasingly difficult for Episcopal and Anglican churches to attract members. With each passing generation fewer people are interested in church. It used to be assumed that people were 'spiritual but not religious,' but that is being replaced by 'spiritual but secular' – meaning that organized religion is no longer an option for people. How does the church navigate a culture where there is increasingly little interest in organized religion?

In a post-modern world, Anglicans will need to become cultural anthropologists – knowing and studying culture with the same passion that we know and study the Bible. Being market savvy does not mean selling out the Gospel or our Anglican heritage, but it does mean communicating the time-tested truths of our faith in ways that connect with a rapidly changing culture: where pluralism and relativism are celebrated, learning is endless, all systems are viewed as alienating and repressive, all authorities are suspect, and reality is kaleidoscopic, organic, multicultural and chaotic. How then, does one proclaim the Gospel in a world where there is no objective truth and all explanations of reality are constructs? How can a Christian say that "Jesus is Lord" without appearing to be a bigot?

While maintaining the essentials of our Anglican heritage, the church must somehow adapt to a new, emerging world and touch hearts and minds with the Gospel of God's love in Jesus. We must preach and teach the Bible, worship in the beauty of holiness, and continue to value the rich heritage that is Anglicanism, but we must also build bridges with a culture that does not necessarily know the Christian story or sing the Lord's song as we do. In a way, we are all missionaries now, with the mission field right outside our doors.

The good news is that the church does not have to reinvent the wheel to engage in worship evangelism. There are entrepreneurial churches already effectively ministering in a secular, postmodern world, and some of these are Episcopal and Anglican churches that have solid core beliefs and values in their message while being flexible and adaptable in their methods. You can be a traditional church with classic Anglican theology and still appeal to seekers. A church of roots and wings is grounded in time-tested biblical truth and able to meet people at their own level of need and understanding. It is not a matter of either/or but doing both.

Here are just some of the transitions that we will need to make as we move from a traditional to an entrepreneurial church:

1. From minimizing the miraculous to being open to the supernatural.
2. From liberal rationalism to heart and mystery.
3. From linear to non-linear thinking.
4. From print to image.
5. From centralized authority to disbursed authority.
6. From top-down decision-making to bottom-up decision-making.
7. From low touch/ low tech to high touch/ high tech.
8. From tradition determines style to mission shapes style.
9. From closed boundaries to open parameters.
10. From sacred space to sacred moments
11. From eternal life to abundant life.
12. From a generic God to a focus on the Holy Trinity.
13. From knowing about God to experiencing God.
14. From expecting people to come to church to engaging people in their communities.
15. From one size fits all to choices and options.
16. From religion to relationships.
17. From 'believing leads to belonging' to 'belonging leads to believing'.
18. From "what is true?" to "what works for me?"
19. From rules and regulations to love and grace.
20. From apologetics to personal testimony.
21. From worship for believers only to worship for believers and seekers.
22. From membership to discipleship.
23. From church as a destination to church as a way station.
24. From inhabiting to journeying.
25. From Christianity as a belief system to Christianity as an experience with Jesus.
26. From individualism to connection, conversation and community.
27. From an insular mindset to an outreach orientation.
28. From Sunday morning to a seven-day-a-week church.
29. From judgment and condemnation to seeing the good in every human being.
30. From expecting seekers to meet church standards to accepting seekers as they are.

31. From doom and gloom to giving people hope for a new and better tomorrow.
32. From abstract and nebulous sermons to meeting people at their point of need and understanding.
33. From giving people information to transforming lives in Jesus.
34. From knowing about God to knowing God.
35. From faith as belief to faith as trust.

Effective evangelism in a twenty-first century world does not mean that Anglicans need to compromise on what is essential to Christian faith. It is not our message but our methods that need to change. Entrepreneurial imagination and energy must be balanced by confidence in preaching and teaching the Bible, holding to the fundamentals of our Anglican heritage, and engaging in Gospel ministry that reaches out to people beyond our membership with the same love and acceptance that our great God has for us.

One of the mistakes of new liturgies is the emphasis on the immanent rather than the transcendent. Whatever the difficulties of the 1662 Prayer Book, you cannot worship from that book and not have a deep sense of holiness, sanctity, reverence and solemnity based on God's majestic power and abiding love. Worship and adoration, thanks and praise, offering "our souls and bodies, to be a reasonable, holy, and living sacrifice" to God is the result of such worship. Too often, by contrast, contemporary liturgies are flat, didactic, verbose and reflect a World Religions 101 course. These liturgies neither edify nor inspire but indoctrinate a way that may not be fully Christian. Could it be that American Episcopalians and Canadian Anglicans are losing members because they have, in marketing terms, lost their brand, moving away from classical Anglicanism into a vacuous, spiritual wasteland?

Anglicans will need a clear biblical message and a coherent evangelism strategy to minister effectively in a twenty-first century world. They also will require effectively trained clergy and lay workers who are Christ-centered, prayerful, able teachers and preachers of the Bible with the ability to minister in a secular, post-modern world where the church is on the margins rather than at the center of cultural life. Clergy must be skilled parish leaders who can maximize biblical literacy and Christian maturity among members of their congregations. They will not only be pastors to their own members but seek out non-members, developing relationships, building trust, and engaging with the surrounding community. They will take to heart the maxim of Archbishop William Temple that "the Church exists for the benefit of those who do not belong to its membership." As theologian Peter Adam put it, the task of church leaders is "not to serve themselves in ministry, or to win the approval of others, or to climb the ladder of hierarchy, but to live and minister to an audience of one, namely God."[1] They will be followers of Jesus and loyal to the Gospel, above all else.

> Growing Anglican churches will communicate a whole Gospel for the whole world, being ready to meet people at their own level of need and understanding, offering the good news in terms and forms that relate to their situation, that speak to them in their language and their cultural style, addressing their existential questions from a biblical perspective. These churches will help people discover for themselves the significance of Jesus Christ in a nurturing and non-threatening environment, using today's technology to maximize communications, and being willing to explore the tough issues of Christian faith with an open mind and non-judgmental love. They will practice a method of evangelism commended by D.T. Niles: "one beggar telling another beggar where to find bread."

The Prayer Book has an important role in evangelizing our culture. There is serious, substantive truth in the Prayer Book that people need, even if they are not aware of it. St. Augustine prayed, "Our hearts are restless until they rest in thee." The ache of the human heart, the pain and loneliness of so many will not be satisfied by superficial pap, or self-help maxims, or three steps to a better life. The church – and only the church – is commissioned by Jesus to fulfill that most basic need of every human being, the need for a relationship with God. Anglicans will refuse to offer a self-help gospel in which God meets our needs, makes us happy and our lives free of trouble. Rather Anglicans will acknowledge that the spiritual journey is rewarding but not easy. It will stretch us, challenge us, ask us to look at ourselves, examine our lives, take stock of who we are and what we do, repent of our sins, what we have done and left undone, and amend our lives, confident that God's love in Jesus is for everyone, everywhere, without exception.

## III. An Anglican Future

*The Book of Common Prayer* is a gift to the world, but its future is uncertain. Will there continue to be one book or a proliferation of books: a Sunday service book; a book of Daily Prayer; a book of Pastoral Offices; a seasonal resource book? Or will the church move beyond common prayer altogether and simply settle for a common structure of worship with multiple options that will allow for a whole range of worship styles and theologies from classical and traditional to contemporary and seeker?

One book, many books, or no book is the question. While no one can answer this question definitely, we do have glimpses of what an Anglican future will look like. How the Prayer Book fits into this future will be a matter of ongoing discussion and discernment. Here are five pillars for any future Prayer Book.

1.  **Christ at the Center.** Bishop Michael Marshall was fond of saying that the church is a community of people who have nothing in common except Jesus Christ in whom they have all things in common. In an increasingly diverse church, Anglicans will find their unity in Christ to whom the Bible and the historic creeds bear witness. This Christ-centeredness will allow the church to have unity in essentials and liberty in non-essentials. We will express this Christ-centeredness through worship, prayer, study, and service, with the Prayer Book playing a central role in our focus on Christ.

2.  **Catholic and Reformed.** Whatever the cultural upheavals ahead, Anglicans will maintain continuity with the church throughout history. At the same time Anglicans will stand firm on the principle of the English Reformation: to add nothing to the ancient faith of the church; to take nothing away from it; and not to define too exactly those mysteries which God has hidden

in God's own knowledge. Moreover, the reformed character of Anglicanism recognizes all truth is incomplete and provisional, and that the church is not perfect but in constant need of reform. The meaning of the scriptures is never exhausted, for there is always more light and truth to be found, whether in the church or the world. Conclusions arrived at by human reason even with the guidance of the Holy Spirit are always open to amendment.

3. **A Comprehensive Church.** Anglicanism will continue to value the distinctive insights of each tradition within the church: catholic, evangelical, liberal and charismatic. These traditions inform and complement one another and produce an unrivaled richness in ways of understanding and expressing the grace of God. The church will continue to be practical rather than confessional, emphasizing pragmatism over doctrinal rigidity, including in any new Prayer Book. At the same time, there will be an appeal to Scripture, the historic teachings of the church and our Anglican heritage, but balanced by theological comprehensiveness, allowing a wide latitude of interpretation in matters of doctrine, and being hesitant to define too precisely disputed matters of faith.

4. **An Outreach Orientation.** Anglicans will find ways to remain a Prayer Book church while engaging in worship evangelism – helping seekers and non-believers to experience God at their own level of need and understanding, and at whatever stage of their spiritual journey. In a post-modern and post-Christian world, Anglicans will focus not just on themselves or those who come to church, or even those who consider themselves Christian. Instead they will live out the 'parish principle' of a commitment to people both within and outside the community of faith, finding ways of worship that will resonate and connect to a generation that may not even know the Lord at all.

5. **Ecumenical and International.** Anglicans will be committed to the catholic or universal character of the church, fostering relations with other churches, engaging in theological dialogue, learning new ways of worship, and working in common mission. Meaningful dialogue allows the church to pursue the truth openly while never claiming to possess it definitively. Truth is always

greater than our understanding of it. Moreover, the three-legged stool of scripture, reason and tradition has now in contemporary Anglicanism a fourth leg which is experience: a readiness to adapt to changing circumstances and a willingness to revise accepted norms in light of contemporary knowledge and experience. This makes Anglicanism not only pastoral and liturgical but dialogical, with a willingness to engage with the 'other' without fear, defensiveness or trepidation. This willingness to engage with the other should apply to churches without the historic episcopate. While the historic episcopate has been deemed a basis for unity by Resolution 11 of the Lambeth Conference of 1888, the resolution goes on to say that the episcopate may be "locally adapted in the methods of its administration to the varying needs of the nations and peoples called of God into the Unity of His Church." In other words, there is flexibility in the shape and practice of the episcopate, whether monarchial, representative or democratic.

The ongoing liturgical life of the church is fluid and in process, shaped by prayer, experience and reflection. Twenty-first century Anglicanism will be a movement in progress – "a church reformed, always reforming." However, with so much change, this much is certain: the churches of the Anglican Communion will continue to order their worship in ways that proclaim the good news of God's love in Jesus to a world so desperately in need of that love.

## Questions

1. Of the ten characteristics of Prayer Book worship, name one or two that you value the most. Are there any that you value least? Explain your answer.

2. Given the technological revolution today, the increasing doctrinal and liturgical pluralism within the church, and the challenges of ministering in a post-Christian culture, how does a printed, bound copy of the Prayer Book fit into this new, emerging world?

3. Is the use of traditional or "religious sounding language" a help or hindrance to you in public worship? Explain your answer.

# FINAL REFLECTIONS

In my years of parish ministry, one of the most common reactions from newcomers about *The Book of Common Prayer* is how the words in some unexplainable way lift their heart to the divine mystery that is God. Some people who know little or nothing about the Episcopal Church or even Christianity will tell me how the Prayer Book comforted them in the face of tragedy, or strengthened them to deal with the challenges ahead, or inspired them to rethink their relationship with God. Some people are not at all sure what they believe, but in the Prayer Book they find words that resonate with them, speak to them at their deepest level of need and understanding, and help them believe that at the heart of the universe is a not a black hole that sucks the life out of us but the light and love of God.

*The Book of Common Prayer* allows Anglicans to take in all kinds of people, believers, seekers, doubters, the half-hearted and the half-committed. There is no test of conscience in Anglicanism, no requirement that people believe exactly the same things in the same way. As long as you share with us in our worship, you are welcome. This is more than merely sensible. It is Christian. It is in line with some of the most readily self-authenticating things in the record of what Jesus said. "Come to me, all you that are weary and are carrying heavy burdens, and I will give you rest" (Mt. 11:28, NRSV). It is a small paradigm of the mercy of God.

Long before anyone spoke words like 'inclusive' or 'comprehensive,' Archbishop Thomas Cranmer was trying to bring the people of England together in the use of one worship book. The 1549 *Book of Common Prayer* was designed to appeal to both Catholics and Protestants. Cranmer was very deliberate in including many traditional prayers and collects of the church that he translated and in some cases revised from the Latin. He did not want to discard old liturgies but to include them so long as they were not contrary to Scripture. Cranmer's liturgical reform did not throw out the baby with the bathwater, as the saying goes. He did not want to clean house so thoroughly that he discarded all the furniture. His was a reform, not a revolution – what today we would term 'liturgical renewal' – breathing new life into old forms of worship: including, revising and discarding material as necessary, but maintaining continuity between past and present.

Nothing better indicates this intent to connect past with present than the maintenance of bishops, priests and deacons. Calvin, Zwingli and other continental reformers abolished the Threefold Order of Ministry. Luther was more indifferent to the matter, but since he and Melanchthon lacked the bishops to support their cause except in Sweden and possibly other Nordic countries, they settled for a church with pastors only. How different is the Church of England! Even with the most reformed Prayer Book of 1552, the church was intent, as indicated by the preface to the Ordinal, to maintain the historic ministry of bishops, priests and deacons. Most Puritans hated the Threefold Ministry and wanted it abolished or at least radically reformed, but Anglicans firmly resisted such attempts, until a climax came in 1662 when all clergy who refused episcopal ordination were removed from their parishes. On the issue of episcopal ordination, Anglicans drew a line in the sand and held to it. We may regret that intransigent stance since many outstanding Puritan ministers were ejected from parishes. However, it showed the firm resolve of Anglicans to maintain Catholic polity, even at a tragic personal cost.

And yet, the Anglican anomaly is that the Church of England maintained Catholic polity along with a doctrinal moderate Calvinism. The *1552 Book of Common Prayer* was not a minor episode in Anglicanism, even though its existence lasted less than a year. That same Prayer Book, with some very minor changes, was accepted in 1559, confirmed in 1604, and finally solidified in 1662. Keep in mind that in 1559, Queen Elizabeth and church leaders had a choice. They could have reverted back to the 1549 Prayer Book or stayed with the 1552 book. Returning to the 1549 book might have placated some of Elizabeth's Catholic subjects, but it would have disheartened church leaders, almost all of whom were of the Reformed persuasion. When the choice between two different books was put before the Queen and church leaders, the 1552 book was clearly preferred as best reflecting the doctrine and faith of the church. While there were minor changes in the 1559 book, such as combining the words of administration of the sacrament, the removal of the Black Rubric and a disparaging reference to the Bishop of Rome in the Great Litany, on all essential matters – including the prayer of preparation by the priest before reception of communion (whether it was a consecration of the elements or not is a matter of debate) – the church clearly preferred the 1552 book.

If there is any question about the theology of the 1559 Prayer Book, or for that matter the 1662 Prayer Book, one need only go to the Thirty-nine Articles of Religion which were adopted in 1563 and finalized in 1571. Look to the Articles to interpret the Prayer Book. The Articles are the only authoritative statement of faith that the Church of England has ever produced. Unlike many of the continental European statements of faith – Zwingli's Sixty-Seven Articles (1523), the First Confession of Basel (1534), the Helvetic Confessions (1536, 1562), the Geneva Confession (1536), the Lausanne Articles (1536), the Augsburg Confession (1530), the Formula of Concord (1577), and the decrees and canons of the Council of Trent (1545 – 1563), the Thirty-nine Articles are deliberately concise. They reflect a moderate Calvinism which itself is reflected in the *1662 Book of Common Prayer.*

After the 1662 Prayer Book was officially approved, it was common to say that the Church of England had a papist liturgy and Calvinist articles. There is some truth in this, but it is not entirely correct. In structure, the Communion rite was in many ways similar to the Roman Catholic Mass. While the elements of bread and wine were set apart and took on a special significance that they did not possess in 1552, the consecration prayer was immediately followed by reception of the elements. The consecration was not the climax of the liturgy as with the Roman Catholic Mass. Rather it was reception of the elements by faith. Attendance at Mass had become reception of Holy Communion.

The Scottish Prayer Book of 1764 and the American Episcopal Prayer Book of 1789 reverted back to the 1549 Prayer of Consecration, and so in those churches to this day there is more of a sense of the real presence of Christ in the bread and wine and a recognition that the Communion is a memorial of Christ's sacrifice on the cross. The Articles of Religion have not played as important a role in these churches as in the Church of England. Moreover, American Episcopalians are much more likely to take umbrage at being called Protestants. They prefer to think of themselves as Catholics, liberal Catholics, evangelical Catholics or reformed Catholics – Catholic without the Pope, as Bishop Stephen Gardiner originally thought of the Church of England.

There always will be a Prayer Book in the churches of the Anglican Communion. In an age where the Articles of Religion lack the doctrinal authority of previous generations, the Prayer Book is the foundational witness in Anglicanism of biblical faith and worship. The genius of Anglicanism is that it has managed to be in continuity with the church of past ages but has never sought to exclude Christians who would be part of it in the present. The Prayer Book has been the chief instrument of comprehensiveness that has brought disparate people together in common worship.

In future Prayer Books, the challenge is to maintain this balance of past and present, holding fast to the faith 'once for all' delivered to the saints, but welcoming and embracing a new generation with issues unimaginable to the English reformers. If the underlying theology in our Prayer Books veers too far away from the reformed Catholicism of classical Anglicanism, then we risk ceasing to be a church of common prayer. Bishop Tom Wright has rightly remarked that "the church must be marked both by historical continuity and by a readiness to submit to God's judgment, to admit error, to sit under the Word and learn fresh truth from it."[1] There must be room for all in the church without compromising what is essential to who we are as Anglicans. As I say, this is a delicate balance with no easy solutions but it is the challenge of the church today.

Thankfully, the 1662 Prayer Book continues to be established by law in England, and the 1962 Canadian *Book of Common Prayer* remains the official worship book of Canadian Anglicans, even if some clergy dislike it. Australia, New Zealand and other churches of the Anglican Communion also have official Prayer Books similar to that of the 1662 book, though alternative worship books are commonly used. Even in the Anglican Ordinate of the Roman Catholic Church, much of the beauty and transcendence of Anglican worship remains in their worship books, albeit with Cranmerian language but non-Cranmerian Eucharistic theology.

It has been said that the church is always one generation away from extinction. The same could be said of the Prayer Book. It is up to the churches of the Anglican Communion to maintain the rich deposit of faith contained in their books and to pass it on to future generations. We may need to update the language – just as the English reformers transitioned the church from Latin to English – but the underlying theology, a reformed Catholicism, remains valid, relevant, and above all, true.

I close with the words of Bishop T.W. Drury, whose brief book titled *How We Got Our Prayer Book*, remains a classic for all students of Anglicanism. He wrote his book in 1901 when there was great optimism about the future of the church and the opportunities for mission around the world. We live in a far different world today, and few, if any of us, would have the temerity to refer to the twenty-first century as "the Christian Century." And yet, the mission of the church given to us by Jesus has not changed. The risen Christ has charged us: "Go therefore and make disciples of all nations, baptizing them in the name of the Father and of the Son and of the Holy Spirit, and teaching them to obey everything that I have commanded you" (Mt. 28:19-20, NRSV). We carry out this mission in the assurance that Jesus is with us always and forever because he has told us: "I am with you always, to the end of the age" (Mt. 28:20, NRSV).

We in the twenty-first century need to regain that boundless hope that was present at the beginning of the twentieth century and recommit ourselves to set the world on fire with the good news of God's transforming love in Jesus. Our circumstances are far different, but the mission remains the same. The Gospel message is unchanging even as our methods of ministry will always be changing. An innovative, entrepreneurial spirit will combine with biblical truth, gospel ministry and our Anglican heritage. If we are grounded in the historic faith of the church, we can soar into the future with boldness and confidence. To quote Bishop Drury:

> If only the sons and daughters of our church are found living lives true to the spiritual principles of Scripture as unfolded in our Prayer Book, not only will the Church of England be found a great deal stronger than some folks wish her to be, not only will she continue to be the great bulwark of Protestantism in Europe, and an increasing blessing in our own land, but she will be stronger to carry the Gospel to other lands, to win the whole world for Christ, and to hasten the coming of the kingdom of God.[2]

I echo that hope for the twenty-first century church in North America. May it be so, dear, God, may it be so!

# APPENDIX

## AN UPDATED AND CONDENSED VERSION OF THE ORDER FOR THE ADMINISTRATION OF THE LORD'S SUPPER OR HOLY COMMUNION ACCORDING TO THE 1552 BOOK OF COMMON PRAYER

*The Table having at the Communion time a fair white line cloth upon it, shall stand in the body of the church, or in the chancel, where Morning Prayer or Evening Prayer be appointed to be said.*

*And the Priest standing at the North Side of the Table, shall say The Lord's Prayer, with this Collect following.*

Almighty God, unto whom all hearts be open, all desires known, and from whom no secrets are hid: cleanse the thoughts of our hearts by the inspiration of thy holy spirit, that we may perfectly love thee, and worthily magnify thy holy name: through Christ our Lord. **Amen.**

*Then shall the Priest rehearse distinctly all the Ten Commandments: and the people kneeling, shall after every Commandment ask God's mercy for their transgressions of the same, after this sort.*

God spake these words and said: I am the Lord thy God: Thou shalt have none other gods but me.
**Lord, have mercy upon us, and incline our hearts to keep thy law.**

Thou shalt not make to thy self any graven image, nor the likeness of anything that is in the heaven above, or in the earth beneath, or in the water under the earth; thou shalt not bow down to them, nor worship them.
**Lord, have mercy upon us, and incline our hearts to keep thy law.**

Thou shalt not take the name of the Lord thy God in vain.
**Lord, have mercy upon us, and incline our hearts to keep thy law.**

Remember that thou keep holy the Sabbath day.
**Lord, have mercy upon us, and incline our hearts to keep thy law.**

Honor thy father and thy mother, that thy days may be long in the land which the Lord thy God giveth thee.
**Lord, have mercy upon us, and incline our hearts to keep thy law.**

Thou shalt do no murder.
**Lord, have mercy upon us, and incline our hearts to keep thy law.**

Thou shalt not commit adultery.
**Lord, have mercy upon us, and incline our hearts to keep thy law.**

Thou shalt not steal.
**Lord, have mercy upon us, and incline our hearts to keep thy law.**

Thou shalt not bear false witness against thy neighbor.
**Lord, have mercy upon us, and incline our hearts to keep thy law.**

Thou shalt not covet thy neighbor's house, thou shalt not covet thy neighbor's wife, nor his servant, nor his maid, nor his ox, nor his ass, nor anything that is his.
**Lord, have mercy upon us, and write all these thy laws in our hearts, we beseech thee.**

*Then shall follow the Collect of the day: the Priest standing up and saying.*

Let us pray.

*Immediately after the Collect, the Priest shall
read THE EPISTLE, beginning thus.*

The Epistle written in the _____Chapter of _____.

*And the Epistle ended, he shall say the Gospel beginning thus.*

The Gospel written in the _____Chapter of_____.

*And the Epistle and Gospel being ended, shall be said the CREED.*

**I believe in one God, the Father Almighty, maker of heaven and earth, and of all things visible and invisible.**

**And in one Lord, Jesus Christ, the only-begotten Son of God, begotten of his Father before all worlds, God of God, Light of Light, very God of very God, begotten, not made, being of one substance with the Father, by whom all things were made: who for us men and for our salvation came down from heaven, and was incarnate by the Holy Ghost of the Virgin Mary, and was made man, and was crucified also for us under Pontius Pilate. He suffered and was buried; and the third day he rose again according to the Scriptures, and ascended into heaven, and sitteth on the right hand of the Father; and he shall come again with glory to judge both the quick and the dead; whose kingdom shall have no end.**

**And I believe in the Holy Ghost, the Lord and giver of life, who proceedeth from the Father and the Son, who with the Father and the Son together is worshipped and glorified, who spake by the Prophets.**

**And I believe one Catholic and Apostolic church. I acknowledge one Baptism for the remission of sins. And I look for the resurrection of the dead, and the life of the world to come. Amen.**

*After the Creed, if there be no sermon, shall follow one of the homilies already set forth, or hereafter to be set forth by common authority.*

*After such sermon, homily or exhortation, the Curate shall declare unto the people whether there be any holy days or fasting days the week following; and earnestly exhort them to remember the poor, saying one or more of these Sentences following, as he think most convenient by his discretion.*

Let your light so shine before men, that they may see your good works, and glorify your Father which is in heaven.

Whatsoever you would that men should do unto you, even so do unto them: for this the Law and the Prophets.

Charge them that are rich in this world, that they be ready to give, and glad to distribute, laying up in store for themselves a good foundation against the time to come, that they may attain eternal life.

Give alms of thy goods, and never turn thy face from any poor man, and then the face of the Lord shall not be turned away from thee.

*(There are many other sentences provided.)*

*Then shall the Churchwardens, or some other by them appointed, gather the devotion of the people, and put the same into the poor man's box: and upon the offering days appointed, every man and woman shall pay to the curate the due and accustomed offerings: after which done the priest shall say.*

Let us pray for the whole state of Christ's Church militant here on earth.

Almighty and everlasting God, which by the holy Apostle hast taught us to make prayers and supplications, and to give thanks for all men. We humbly beseech thee mercifully to accept our alms and to receive these our prayers, which we offer unto thy divine Majesty, beseeching thee to inspire continually the universal church with the spirit of truth, unity and concord: And grant that all they that do confess thy holy name, may agree in the truth of thy holy word, and live in unity and godly love.

We beseech thee also to save and defend all Christian Kings, Princes and Governors, and especially thy servant Edward our King, that under him we may be godly and quietly governed: and grant unto his whole council, and to all that be put in authority under him, that they may truly and indifferently administer justice, to the punishment of wickedness and vice, and to the maintenance of God's true religion and virtue.

Give grace, O heavenly Father, to all Bishops, Pastors and Curates, that they may both by their life and doctrine set forth thy true and lively word, and rightly and duly administer thy holy Sacraments: and to all thy people give thy heavenly grace, and especially to this congregation here present, that with meek heart and due reverence they may hear and receive thy holy word, truly serving thee in holiness and righteousness all the days of their life.

And we humbly beseech thee of thy goodness, O Lord, to comfort and succor all them, which in this transitory life be in trouble, sorrow, need, sickness or any other adversity.

Grant this, O Father, for Jesus Christ's sake, our only mediator and advocate. **Amen.**

*Exhortations are then said to bid people who are negligent to come to the holy Communion.*

*Then shall the Priest say to them that come to receive holy Communion.*

Ye that do truly and earnestly repent you of your sins, and be in love and charity with your neighbors, and intend to lead a new life, following the commandments of God, and walking henceforth in his holy ways: Draw near and take this holy Sacrament to your comfort: make your humble confession to almighty God, before this congregation here gathered together in his holy name, meekly kneeling upon your knees.

*Then shall this general confession be made, in the name of all those that are mindful to receive the holy Communion, either by one of them, or else by one of the ministers, or by the Priest himself, all kneeling humbly upon their knees.*

Almighty God, Father of our Lord Jesus Christ, maker of all things, judge of all men, we acknowledge and bewail our manifold sins and wickedness, which we from time to time most grievously have committed, by thought, word and deed, against thy divine Majesty: provoking most justly thy wrath and indignation against us: we do earnestly repent, and be heartily sorry for these our misdoings: the remembrance of them is grievous unto us, the burden of them is intolerable: have mercy upon us, have mercy upon us, most merciful Father, for thy Son our Lord Jesus Christ's sake: forgive us all that is past, and grant that we may ever here after serve and please thee, in newness of life, to the honor and glory of thy name; through Jesus Christ our Lord.

*Then shall the Priest or the Bishop (being present) stand up, and turning himself to the people, say thus,*

Almighty God, our heavenly Father, who of his great mercy, hath promised forgiveness of sins to all them, which with hearty repentance and true faith turn unto him: have mercy upon you, pardon and deliver you from all your sins, confirm and strengthen you in all goodness and bring you to everlasting life; through Jesus Christ our Lord. **Amen.**

*Then shall the Priest also say,*

Hear what comfortable words our Savior Christ saith, to all that truly turn to him.

>Come unto me all that travail, and be heavy laden, and I shall refresh you. So God loved the world, that he gave his only begotten Son to the end that all that believe in him, should not perish, but have life everlasting.

Hear also what St. Paul saith.

>This is a true saying, and worthy of all men to be received, that Jesus Christ came into the world to save sinners.

Hear also what St. John saith.

>If any man sin, we have an advocate with the Father, Jesus Christ the righteous, and he is the propitiation for our sins.

*After the which the Priest shall proceed, saying,*

Lift up your hearts.
**We lift them up unto the Lord.**
Let us give thanks unto our Lord God.
**It is meet and right so to do.**

It is very meet, right and our bounden duty, that we should at all times, and in all places, give thanks unto thee, O Lord, holy Father, almighty and everlasting God.

*(Here shall follow the proper Preface according to the time.*
*After which preface shall follow immediately,)*

Therefore with Angels and Archangels, and with all the company of heaven, we laud and magnify thy glorious Name, evermore praising thee and saying:

**Holy, holy, holy, Lord God of hosts,**
**Heaven and earth are full of thy glory;**
**glory be to thee, O Lord most High.**

*Then shall the Priest, kneeling down at God's board, say in the name*
*of all them that shall receive the Communion, this prayer following.*

We do not presume to come to this thy table, O merciful Lord, trusting in our own righteousness, but in thy manifold and great mercies. We be not worthy so much as to gather up the crumbs under thy table, but thou art the same Lord, whose property is always to have mercy: grant us therefore, gracious Lord, so to eat the flesh of thy dear Son Jesus Christ, and to drink his blood, that our sinful bodies may be made clean by his body, and our souls washed by his most precious blood, and that we may evermore dwell in him and he in us. **Amen.**

*Then the Priest standing up shall say, as followeth.*

Almighty God, our heavenly Father, which of thy tender mercy didst give thine only Son Jesus Christ to suffer death upon the Cross for our redemption, who made there, by his one oblation of himself once offered, a full, perfect and sufficient sacrifice, oblation and satisfaction for the sins of the whole world; and did institute, and in his holy Gospel command us to continue, a perpetual memory of that his precious death, until his coming again.

Hear us, O merciful Father, we beseech thee, and grant that we receiving these thy creatures of bread and wine, according to thy Son our Savior Jesus Christ's holy institution, in remembrance of his death and passion, may be partakers of his most blessed body and blood:

Who, in the same night that he was betrayed, took bread, and when he had given thanks, he brake it, and gave it to his disciples, saying, "Take, eat; this is my body, which is given for you: do this in remembrance of me."

Likewise after supper he took the cup, and when he had given thanks, he gave it to them, saying, "Drink ye all of this; for this is my blood of the New Testament, which is shed for you and for many for the remission of sins: do this, as oft as ye shall drink it, in remembrance of me."

*Then shall the minister first receive the Communion in both kinds himself, and next deliver it to other ministers, if any be there present (that they may help the chief minister) and after to the people in their hands kneeling.*

*And when he delivereth the bread, he shall say.*

Take and eat this, in remembrance that Christ died for thee, and feed on him in thy heart by faith, with thanksgiving.

*And the Minister that delivereth the cup shall say,*

Drink this in remembrance that Christ's blood was shed for thee, and be thankful.

*Then shall the Priest say the Lord's Prayer, the people repeating after every petition.*

Our Father, which art in heaven, hallowed be thy name. Thy kingdom come. Thy will be done in earth as it is in heaven. Give us this day our daily bread. And forgive us our trespasses, as we forgive them that trespass against us. And lead us not into temptation. But deliver us from evil. Amen.

*After shall be said as followeth.*

O Lord and heavenly Father, we thy humble servants entirely desire thy fatherly goodness mercifully to accept this our Sacrifice of praise and thanksgiving: most humbly beseeching thee to grant, that by the merits and death of thy Son Jesus Christ, and through faith in his blood, we and all thy whole church may obtain remission of our sins, and all other benefits of his Passion.

And here we offer and present unto thee, O Lord, our selves, our souls and bodies, to be a reasonable, holy and lively Sacrifice unto thee; humbly beseeching thee that all we, which be partakers of this holy Communion, may be fulfilled with thy grace and heavenly benediction.

And although we be unworthy, through our manifold sins, to offer unto thee any Sacrifice, yet we beseech thee to accept this our bounden duty and service, not weighing our merits, but pardoning our offences, through Jesus Christ our Lord;

By whom, and with whom, in the unity of the Holy Ghost, all honor and glory be unto thee, O Father Almighty, world without end. **Amen.**

*Or this.*

Almighty and ever-living God, we most heartily thank thee, for that thou dost vouchsafe to feed us, which have duly received these holy mysteries, with the spiritual food of the most precious body and blood of thy Son our Savior Jesus Christ, and dost assure us thereby of thy favor and goodness toward us, and that we be very members incorporate in the mystical body, which is the blessed company of all faithful people, and be also heirs, through hope, of thy everlasting kingdom, by the merits of the most precious death and passion of thy dear Son. We now most humbly beseech thee, O heavenly Father, so to assist us with thy grace, that we may continue in that holy fellowship and do all such good works, as thou hast prepared for us to walk in; through Jesus Christ our Lord, to whom, with thee and the Holy Ghost, be all honor and glory, world without end. **Amen.**

*That shall be said or sung.*

**Glory be to God on high, and in earth peace, good will towards men. We praise thee, we bless thee, we worship thee, we glorify thee, we give thanks to thee for thy great glory, O Lord God, heavenly king, God the Father almighty.**

**O Lord, the only-begotten Son, Jesus Christ; O Lord God, Lamb of God, Son of the Father, that takest away the sins of the world, have mercy upon us; thou that takest away the sins of the world, have mercy upon us; thou that takest away the sins of the world, receive**

our prayer; thou that sittest at the right hand of God the Father, have mercy upon us.

For thou only art holy; thou only art the Lord; thou only, O Christ, with the Holy Ghost, art most high in the glory of God the Father. Amen.

*Then the Priest, or the Bishop if be present, shall
let them depart with this blessing:*

The peace of God, which passeth all understanding keep your hearts and minds in the knowledge and love of God, and of his Son Jesus Christ our Lord: And the blessing of God almighty, the Father, the Son, and the Holy Ghost, be amongst you and remain with you always. **Amen.**

*And there shall be no celebration of the Lord's Supper, except there be a
good number to communicate with the Priest, according to his discretion.*

*And to take away the superstition, which any person hath, or might
have in the bread and wine, it shall suffice that the bread be such as
is usual to be eaten at the Table with other meats, but the best and
purest wheat bread, that conveniently may be gotten. And if any of
the bread or wine remain, the Curate shall have it to his own use.*

*And note, that every Parishioner shall communicate, at least three
times in the year, of which Easter to be one: and shall also receive the
Sacraments, and other rites, according to the order in this book appointed.
And yearly, at Easter, every Parishioner shall reckon with his Parson, Vicar,
or Curate, or his, or their deputy or deputies, and pay to them or him all
Ecclesiastical duties, accustomably due, then and at that time to be paid.*

*Although no order can be so perfectly devised, but it may be of some,
either for their ignorance and infirmity, or else of malice and obstinacy,
misconstrued, depraved, and interpreted in a wrong part: And yet because
brotherly charity willeth that so much as conveniently may be, offences
should be take away: therefore we willing do the same. Whereas it is
ordained in The Book of Common Prayer, in the administration of the
Lord's Supper, that the communicants kneeling should receive the holy
Communion (which thing be well meant, for a signification of the humble*

*and grateful acknowledging of the benefits of Christ, given unto the worthy receiver, and to avoid the profanation and disorder, which about the holy Communion might else ensue) lest yet the same kneeling might be thought for taken otherwise, we do declare that it is not meant thereby that any adoration is done, or ought to be done, either unto the Sacramental bread or wine there bodily received, or unto any real and essential presence there being of Christ's natural flesh and blood. For as concerning the Sacramental bread and wine, they remain still in their very natural substances, and therefore may not be adored (for that were idolatry to be abhorred of all faithful Christians). And as concerning the natural body and blood of our savior Christ, they are in heaven and not here. For it is against the truth of Christ's true natural body, to be in more places than in one, at one time.*

# NOTES

## Preface

1 Rudolf Otto uses the term in his book *The Idea of the Holy* (Pantianos Classics, 1923) eBook Edition.

2 J.I. Packer, *The Evangelical Identity Problem* (Oxford: Latimer House, 1978) 20-21.

3 Quoted by Nigel Scotland, *Evangelical Anglicans in a Revolutionary Age, 1789 – 1901* (Carlisle, England: Paternoster Press, 2004) 355.

## Introduction

1 Humphrey Prideaux, "A Letter to a Friend relating to the Present Convocation." *Anglicanism,* Paul Elmer More and Frank Leslie Cross, ed. (London: S.P.C.K., 1962) 183.

## Session 1

1 Robert Bellarmine, "Concio 9, probitate Dacorum Ecclesiae." *The Anglican Breviary* (Mount Sinai, NY: Frank Gavin Liturgical Foundation, 1955) E191.

2 T.W. Drury, *How We Got Our Prayer Book* (London: James Nisbett & Co., 1901) 28-29.

3 "An Homily Wherein Is Declared That Common Prayer and Sacraments Ought To Be Ministered In A Tongue That Is Understood Of The Hearers." *The Book of Homilies* (London: The Prayer Book Society, 1852) 334.

## Session 2

1 Tim Patrick, *Anglican Foundations: A Handbook to the Source Documents of the English Reformation* (Oxford: The Latimer Trust, 2018) 47.

2 Nigel Scotland, *The Supper: Cranmer and Communion* (Oxford: The Latimer Trust, 2013) 7.

3 Michael Davies, *Cranmer's Godly Order* (Chawleigh, Devon: Augustine Publishing Company, 1976) 91.

4    Thomas Cranmer, *A Defence of the True and Catholick Doctrine of the Sacrament* (Rochester, Kent: Focus Christian Ministries Trust and Harrison Trust, 1987) Book III, Chapter 13, 161-162.

5    Stephen Gardiner, *A Detection of the Devils Sophistry wherewith he robbeth the unlearned people of the true belief in the most blessed Sacrament of the altar.* Cited by John Murphy, Tudor Historian and Writer, on 19/04/2013, at john-murphy.co.uk.

## Session 3

1    Cranmer, *A Defence of the True and Catholick Doctrine of the Sacrament*, I.II.25.

2    Ibid. II.II.34-35.

3    Id. II.VI.63.

4    Id. III.II.98.

5    Id. III.II.100.

6    Id. V.VI.239-240.

7    Id. II.10.135.

8    Colin Buchanan, *What Did Cranmer Think He Was Doing?* (Bramcote, Notts.: Grove Books, 1977) 22-23.

9    Richard Hooker, *The Laws of Ecclesiastical Polity*, Book VII, Chapter 1. *Anglicanism*, 345-348.

10   Ibid. 349.

11   Quoted in Andrew Atherstone, *The Anglican Ordinal: Gospel Priorities for Church of England Ministry* (London: The Latimer Trust, 2020) 47.

12   Richard Hooker, *The Laws of Ecclesiastical Polity*, Book V, Chapter 73. *Anglicanism*, 369.

13   Andrew Atherstone, *The Anglican Ordinal*, 48.

14   Richard Hooker, *The Laws of Ecclesiastical Polity*, V.67.6 (New York: Everyman's Library, 1954) Vol. II, 322-323.

15   John Cosin, "Historia Transubstantiationis Papalis." *Anglicanism*, 470.

## Session 4

1    Tim Patrick, *Anglican Foundations* (Oxford: The Latimer Trust, 2018) 47.

2    "An Homily on the worthy receiving and reverent esteeming of the Sacrament of the Body and Blood of Christ." *The Book of Homilies* (London: The Prayer Book and Homily Society, 1852) 418.

3    Richard Hooker, *The Laws of Ecclesiastical Polity*, V, Chapter 67.6. (New York: Everyman's Library, 1954) Vol. II, 322-323.

4  Lancelot Andrewes, "A Response to the Apology of Cardinal Bellarmine." *Anglicanism*. 464.

5  John Jewel, *The Apology of the Church of England*, Part II. A Public Domain Book. (London: Cassell and Company, 1888). Kindle Edition by David Price.

6  William Forbes, "Considerationes Modesties' et Pacificate Controversiarum de Justificatione, Purgatories, Invocatione Sanctorum, Christo Media tore et Eucharistia, De Eucharistia." *Anglicanism*, 471.

7  John Donne, "On the Sacrament*," Divine Poems*. Cited by Nigel Scotland, *The Supper: Cranmer and Communion* (Oxford: The Latimer Trust, 2013) 46.

8  Taken from *The History of the Troubles and Trials of... Laud*, Chapter III. *Anglicanism*, 510.

9  Edward Carpenter, *CANTUAR: The Archbishops in their Office* (London: Mowbray, 1997) 191.

## Session 5

1  Quoted in Edward Carpenter, *CANTUAR: The Archbishops in their Office* (London: Mowbray, 1997) 201.

2  Ibid. 203.

3  Buchanan, *What Did Cranmer Think He Was Doing?* 31.

4  James Ussher, "A Sermon Preached before the Commons House of Parliament in St. Margaret's Church at Westminster, the 18th of February 1620." *Anglicanism*, 488.

5  John Cosin, "Historia transubstantiationis Papalis." *Anglicanism*, 468.

6  John Bramhall, "An Answer to M. de la Milletiere." *Anglicanism*, 475.

7  Nathaniel Eaton, "De Fastis Anglicis, sive Calendarium Sacrum." *Anglicanism*, 466.

8  John Selden, "Table Talk, Section LXXXI." *Anglicanism,* 178.

9  Cited by H.R. McAdoo, *Anglican Heritage: Theology and Spirituality* (Norwich: Canterbury Press, 1991) 3.

10  Jeremy Taylor, "A Letter to a Gentleman Seduced to the Church of Rome." *Anglicanism,* 15.

11  Simon Patrick, "An Account of the New Sect of Latitude-Men Together with some Reflections upon the New Philosophy." *Anglicanism*, 12.

## Session 6

1  P.H. Davids, *The Letters of 2 Peter and Jude* (Nottingham: Apollos, 2006) 68-69.

2  The Teaching of the Catholic Church, Karl Rahner, ed. (Staten Island, NY: Alban House, 1967) 281.

3   Bertrand Russell, *A History of Western Philosophy* (New York: A Touchstone Book, 2007) 472.

4   *The Cambridge Companion to Ockham,* Paul Vincent Spade, ed. (Cambridge: Cambridge University Press, 1999) 104.

5   Dale T. Irvin and Scott W. Sunquist, *History of the World Christian Movement, Vol. I: Earliest Christianity to 1453* (Maryknoll, New York: Orbis Books, 2001) 434.

6   Thomas Cranmer, *A Defence of the True and Catholick Doctrine of the Sacrament*, III. XV. 194-195.

7   Ibid. V.I.232.

8   *The Canons and Decrees of the Council of Trent*, H.J. Schroeder, ed. (Charlotte: TAN Books, 1978) 79.

9   Ibid. 79.

10  Id. 79.

11  Id. 79.

12  Id. 80.

13  Id. 80.

14  Id. 80.

15  Id. 80.

16  Id. 151.

17  Id. 151.

18  Id. 151

19  Id. 151.

20  *Catechism of the Council of Trent*, John McHugh and Charles Callan, trans. (New York: Baronius Press, 2018) 237-238.

21  Ibid. 238.

22  Id. 238-239.

23  Pope Pius XII, "Mediator Dei" (1947), *The Teaching of the Catholic Church*, Karl Rahner, ed. (Staten Island, NY: Alba House, 1967)347-349.

24  John Pearson, *An Exposition of the Creed*. Cited in *Anglicanism*, 538.

25  Edward Gee, *The Texts Examined which Papists Cited out of the Bible for the Proof of their Doctrine concerning Seven Sacraments*. Cited in *Anglicanism*, 414.

26  John Donne*, Sermons* VII. 11. 420-428. *One Equal Light: An Anthology of the Writings of John Donne*, compiled and edited by John Moses (Grand Rapids: William B. Eerdmans Publishing Company, 2003).

27  Cranmer, *A Defence of the True and Catholick Doctrine of the Sacrament*, 240.

28  Ibid. 246.

29  *Testimonies to Anglican Teaching on the Eucharistic Oblation by XII Classical Theologians of the Church of England* (London: The Society of St. Peter and St. Paul, 1975).

## Session 7

1   Gerald Bray, *The Faith We Confess: An Exposition of the Thirty-Nine Articles* (London: The Latimer Trust, 2009) 200.
2   Canon G.H. Bourne, "Lord, enthrone in heavenly splendour." *The Book of Common Praise: Being the Hymn Book of the Anglican Church of Canada* (Toronto: The Anglican Book Centre, 1938) Hymn 235, v. 2.
3   *A Catechism Written in Latin by Alexander Nowell... Together With the Same Catechism Translated Into English by Thomas Norton*. Edited for The Parker Society (Cambridge: The University Press, 1853) 215.
4   Canon William Bright, "And now, O Father, mindful of the love." *The Book of Common Praise, Hymn* 221, v. 1.
5   Bishop E.H. Bickersteth, "O Holy Father, who in tender love." *The Book of Common Praise*, Hymn 220, v. 1.
6   *Nowell, Catechism* (Cambridge: The University Press, 1563) 212.

## Session 8

1   William White, *Case of the Episcopal Churches in the United States Considered.* (Philadelphia: David C. Claypoole, 1792) 5. Cited in Ross Hebb, *Samuel Seabury and Charles Inglis* (Madison: Farleigh Dickinson University Press, 2010) 101.
2   Ibid. 102.
3   Peter Victor Marshall, *One, Catholic and Apostolic: Samuel Seabury and the Early Episcopal Church* (New York: Church Publishing, 2004) 65.
4   Hebb, *Samuel Seabury and Charles Inglis*, 102.
5   Samuel Seabury to Rev. Dr. Smith, 15 August 1785. Cited in Hebb, *Samuel Seabury and Charles Inglis*, 107.
6   Ibid. 107.
7   William Smith, Sermon, in Marshall, *One, Catholic and Apostolic*, 151.
8   Hebb, *Samuel Seabury and Charles Inglis*, 61.

## Session 9

1   Thomas Vogan, *The True Doctrine of the Eucharist* (London: Longmans, Green and Co., 1871) 54.
2   Edgar C.S. Gibson, *The Thirty-nine Articles of the Church of England* (London: Methuen & Co., 1897) 664-665.
3   Dom Gregory Dix, *The Shape of the Liturgy* (London: Dacre Press, 1948) 2.

## Session 10

1   Peter Adam, *Thomas Cranmer: Using the Bible to Evangelize the Nations* (London: The Latimer Trust, 2020) 45-46.

## Final Reflections

1   Tom Wright, "Evangelical Anglican Identity: The Connection Between Bible, Gospel and Church." *Anglican Evangelical Identity: Yesterday and Today* (Vancouver: Regent College Publishing, 2008) 103.
2   T.W. Drury, *How We Got Our Prayer Book* (London: James Nisbet & Co., 1901)) 124.

# BIBLIOGRAPHY

## Prayer Books and Worship Resources

**1549 and 1552:** *The First and Second Prayer Books of Edward VI* (London: J.M. Dent & Sons, 1913).

**1552:** *The Second English Prayer Book of 1552: The Order for the Administration of the Lord's Supper or Holy Communion Arranged and Annotated with Modern Spelling for Church Worship* (Elsack, Skipton: The Wanderer, 2002).

**1549, 1559, 1662:** *The Book of Common Prayer: The Texts of 1549, 1559 and 1662),* Brian Cummings, ed. (Oxford: Oxford University Press, 2011).

**1928:** *The Book of Common Prayer as proposed in 1928* (Norwich: Canterbury Press, 2008).

**2021:** *The Book of Common Prayer International Edition* (Downers Grove, Illinois: InterVarsity Press, 2021).

**1928:** *The Book of Common Prayer* (ECUSA) (Greenwich, Connecticut: The Seabury Press, 1952).

**1962:** *The Book of Common Prayer Canada* (Toronto: Anglican Book Centre, 1962).

**1979:** *The Book of Common Prayer* (ECUSA) (New York: Church Publishing, 1979).

**1985:** *The Book of Alternative Services* (Canada) (Toronto: Anglican Book Centre, 1985).

**2000:** *Common Worship: Services and Prayers for the Church of England* (London: Church House Publishing, 2000).

**1955:** *The Anglican Breviary containing the Divine Office according to the General Usages of the Western Church* (Mount Sinai, Long Island, New York: the Frank Gavin Liturgical Foundation, 1998).

**1961:** *Monastic Breviary Matins according to the Holy Rule of Saint Benedict* (Glendale, CO: Lancelot Andrewes Press, 2007).

**1932 and 1963:** *The Monastic Diurnal or Daily Hours of the Monastic Breviary* (Glendale, CO: Lancelot Andrewes Press, 2006).

**2005:** *Daily Prayer for the Church of England* (London: Church House Publishing, 2005).


**Primary and Secondary Sources**

*A Catechism Written in Latin by Alexander Nowell Together with the Same Catechism Translated into English by Thomas Norton.* Edited for The Parker Society (Cambridge: The University Press, 1853).

*Anglicanism,* Paul Elmer Moore and Frank Leslie Cross, ed. (London: S.P.C.K., 1962).

*Eucharistic Liturgies of Edward VI: A Text for Students*, Colin Buchanan, ed. (Brancote, Notts.: Grove Books, 1983).

*One Equall Light: An Anthology of the Writings of John Donne.* Complied and edited by John Moses (Grand Rapids: William B. Eerdmans Publishing Company, 2003).

*Saepio Officio: The Reply of the Archbishops of Canterbury and York to the Letter Apostolicae Curae of Pope Leo XIII* (London: The Church Literature Association, 1977).

*Testimonies To Anglican Teaching on the Eucharistic Oblation By XII Classical Theologians of the Church of England* (London: The Society of St. Peter and St. Paul, 1975).

*The Book of Homilies* (London: The Prayer Book and Homily Society, 1852). A Nashotah House Press facsimile re-print, 2013).

*The Canons and Decrees of the Council of Trent*, H. J. Schroeder, trans. (Charlotte, NC: TAN Books, 1978).

*The Catechism of the Council of Trent*, John A. McHugh and Charles J. Callan, trans. (New York: Baronius Press, 2018).

*The Consolation of God: Great Sermons of Phillips Brooks*. Ellen Wilbur, editor (Grand Rapids: William B. Eerdmans, 2003).

*The Study of Anglicanism*, Stephen Sykes, John Booty, and Jonathan Knight, eds. (London: SPCK / Fortress Press, 1988).

*The Study of Liturgy*, Cheslyn Jones and Edward Yarnold, S.J., eds. (New York: Oxford University Press, 1992).

*The Teaching of the Catholic Church*, Karl Rahner, ed. (Staten Island, NY: Alba House, 1967).

Adam, Peter, *Thomas Cranmer: Using the Bible to Evangelize the Nation* (London: The Latimer Trust, 2020).

_____, *The 'Very Pure Word of God'* (London: The Latimer Trust, 2012).

Atherstone, Andrew, *The Anglican Ordinal: Gospel Priorities for Church of England Ministry* (London: The Latimer Trust, 2020).

Bartlett, David L, *Ministry in the New Testament* (Eugene, Oregon: Wipf and Stock, 2001).

Belloc, Hilaire, *Characters of the Reformation* (San Francisco: Ignatius Press, 2017).

Bray, Gerald, *A Fruitful Exhortation: A Guide to the Homilies* (London: The Latimer Trust, 2014).

_____, *The Faith We Confess* (London: The Latimer Trust, 2009).

Buchanan, Colin, *What Did Cranmer Think He Was Doing?* (Bramcote, Notts.: Grove Books, 1976).

Burkill, Mark, *Dearly Beloved: Building God's People through Morning and Evening Prayer* (London: The Latimer Trust, 2012).

Carpenter, Edward, *CANTUAR* (London: Mowbray, 1997).

Cranmer, Thomas, *A Defence of the True and Catholick Doctrine of the Sacrament* (Rochester, Kent: Focus Christian Ministries Trust and Harrison Trust, 1987).

Davie, Martin, *Lex Orandi, Lex Credendi: Liturgy, Doctrine and Scripture in History and Today* (London: The Latimer Trust, 2019).

Davies, Michael, *Cranmer's Godly Order* (Chawleigh, Devon: Augustine Publishing Company, 1976) 91.

Duffy, Eamon, *Fires of Faith: Catholic England under Mary Tudor* (New Haven: Yale University Press, 2009).

_____, *The Stripping of the Altars: Traditional Religion in England 1400 – 1580* (New Haven: Yale University Press, 2005).

Hebb, Ross N., *Samuel Seabury and Charles Inglis: Two Bishops, Two Churches* (Madison: Fairleigh Dickinson University Press, 2010).

Laporte, Jean-Marc, S.J., "A Spiritual Assessment of Anglican and Protestant Orders: Absolutely Null and Utterly Void?" Unpublished paper delivered on December 10, 2012.

Marshall, Paul Victor, *One, Catholic and Apostolic: Samuel Seabury and the Early Episcopal Church* (New York: Church Publishing, 2004).

McAdoo, H.R., *Anglican Heritage: Theology and Spirituality* (Norwich: The Canterbury Press, 1991).

Null, Ashley, *Divine Allurement: Cranmer's Comfortable Words* (London: The Latimer Trust, 2014).

Packer, J.I. and Beckwith, R. T., *The Thirty-Nine Articles Their Place and Use Today* (Oxford: Latimer House, 19984).

Packer, J.I. and Wright, N.T., *Anglican Evangelical Identity Yesterday and Today* (Vancouver: Regent College Publishing, 2008).

Patrick, Tim, *Anglican Foundations: A Handbook to the Source Documents of the English Reformation* (London: The Latimer Trust, 2018).

Russell, Bertrand, *A History of Western Philosophy* (New York: A Touchstone Book, 1972).

Sargent, Benjamin, *Day By Day: The Rhythm of the Bible in The Book of Common Prayer* (London: The Latimer Trust, 2012).

Scotland, Nigel, *The Supper: Cranmer and Communion* (London: The Latimer Trust, 2013).

# ABOUT THE AUTHOR

Gary Nicolosi is an Episcopal priest and lawyer who has published hundreds of articles, including the recent book *SOULFIRE: Preaching the Church's Message in a Secular, Postmodern World* which details how to communicate the Gospel message in North American culture.

Throughout his years in ordained ministry, Gary has counted people of different religious backgrounds as his friends, colleagues, teachers and mentors. He was greatly influenced by the Jesuits in his undergraduate and graduate studies at Fordham and Georgetown Universities. At Temple University Law School, Gary studied Judaic Law under Professor and Rabbi Aaron Schreiber and assisted with his book. At Trinity College, University of Toronto he studied under Canadian Anglican theologian Dr. Eugene Fairweather and took classes at Wycliffe College with Dr. Oliver O'Donovan and Dr. Alan Hayes. When he studied for his Doctor of Ministry at Pittsburgh Theological Seminary, his thesis adviser was Dr. Harold Scott, the former Executive Presbyter of the Pittsburgh Presbytery, and one of his thesis examiners was Dr. John Rogers of Trinity School for Ministry. At his parish in San Diego County, his friend and colleague was Lutheran Pastor Jack Lindquist, while his mentor was Samir Kafity, the retired Anglican bishop of Jerusalem.

Gary has ministered in both the American Episcopal and Canadian Anglican Churches. He has served as Canon for Ministries at the Cathedral Church of the Nativity in the Diocese of Bethlehem, Pennsylvania, and Congregational Development Officer in the Diocese of British Columbia. Under his leadership St. Bartholomew's Episcopal Church in suburban San Diego County grew from 1,200 to over 2,300 members. He has conducted church growth, stewardship and theological seminars and workshops in twenty-eight dioceses in the United States and Canada, including a 2009 seminar for the Canadian Anglican and Lutheran Bishops in Niagara Falls. In 2011, he wrote an award-winning article on "Open Communion" recognized by the Associated Church Press (U.S.) and the Canadian Church Press. During his time in the Diocese of Huron in Ontario, Canada, he developed a cutting-edge Post-Ordination Training program for newly ordained clergy. He was a participant in the video *The Many Faces of Anglicanism* in preparation for the 1998 Lambeth Conference.

Gary lives in Peoria, Arizona, with his wife Heather and daughter Allison. He is an active priest in the Diocese of Arizona, serving on the Church Disciplinary Board and supplying at parishes. In addition, he does pro bono immigration and veterans law.

.

Printed in Great Britain
by Amazon